THE CAMPUS LIFE

GUIDE TO

DATING

Campus Life Books

THE CAMPUS LIFE
GUIDE TO
DATING
by DIANE EBLE

A DIVISION OF CTi
CampusLife
BOOKS

ZondervanPublishingHouse
Grand Rapids, Michigan
A Division of HarperCollinsPublishers

The Campus Life Guide to Dating
Copyright © 1990 by Campus Life Books, a division of CTi
All rights reserved

Published by Zondervan Publishing House
1415 Lake Drive, S.E., Grand Rapids, Michigan 49506

Library of Congress Cataloging-in-Publication Data

Eble, Diane
    The campus life guide to dating / Diane Eble.
      p. cm.
    Summary: A guide to dating for high schoolers, written from
a Christian perspective.
    ISBN 0-310-71011-1
    1. Youth—Religious life. 2. Teenagers—Religious life.
3. Dating (Social customs)—Religious aspects—Christianity—
Juvenile literature. (1. Dating (Social customs) 2. Christian
life.) I. Title.
BV4531.2.E25   1990
646.7'7—dc20   90–33184
                                                   CIP
                                                   AC

Printed in the United States of America

90 91 92 93 94 / CH / 10 9 8 7 6 5 4 3 2 1

To Gene,
who has proven to me
that the Dream
can become reality.

Contents

Acknowledgments

Many people lent their insights and experiences to this book. Other *Campus Life* editors and writers contributed to certain portions. Chris Lutes helped with the interviews that led to chapters 2, 7, and 8. Jonathan and Marianne Butler wrote "Starting a Conversation," which originally appeared in *Campus Life.*

I'm especially grateful to Tim Stafford, who for over ten years has been answering questions in the "Love, Sex and the Whole Person" column. Many of his insights and practical suggestions on relationships undergird this book, especially in chapters 14, 15, 16, and 18. Material from chapter 17 was adapted from a series of *Campus Life* articles by Jim Long, Jennifer J. Fay, and Billie Jo Flerchinger of King County Rape Relief, and Claudette McShane. And it was Robin Norwood who first defined what it means to "love too much."

Most of all, I'd like to thank the many young people who were willing to share their experiences, opinions, and ideas, through interviews, letters, and surveys. And to Rodney and Cathy Duttweiler, I wish you a wonderful life together as you share your dream.

—*Diane Eble*

Introduction

During my high-school years, dating seemed like a big game—a game in which the rules were never written down. (Although I did come across a book called *How to Get a Teenage Boy and What to Do with Him When You've Got Him.*) I was totally turned off by the superficiality of the dating game.

Some of the people in my high school seemed to know the rules automatically. My cousin Lynn, for example. Though we were very close, we never talked about why it was she always had a boyfriend and I seldom did. She probably didn't know—and I was too embarrassed to ask.

I wasn't the only one. My best friend Claudia, who was very good-looking, nevertheless hadn't quite caught on to the knack of catching a boyfriend.

"Catching a boy (or girl)" seemed very important then. Looking back, though, it strikes me that where we each ended up depended not so much on where (or when) we started dating, but on how we handled choices along the way.

My friend Kelly (names of my friends are changed to protect their privacy) was one of the brightest people in our class, as well as one of the most beautiful. She was also a Christian. She married right after high-school graduation, moved out of state, and tried to finish college. But her husband did not share many of her values, and felt threatened by her education. She never did finish her degree. She is now divorced, living with a man. Her faith consists of, "Things will work out OK somehow in the end." For Kelly, the journey hasn't been very positive.

Another close friend, Ruth, rarely lacked a boyfriend. Unfortunately, she got pregnant and had an abortion. From that point on I watched her self-esteem slip notch by notch. Now she is married to a man who occasionally beats her. She has two children. She struggles to hang on to faith. And she finds it difficult not to continue to run from problems.

But there are hopeful examples, too. There's Debbie, one of the people who helped me come to know Jesus Christ when I was in high school. Debbie always had a vibrant faith which radiated from her personality. She got involved in a Christian group at her college, and met her husband there. Now she is married with three kids. She and her husband share a strong mutual faith that enables them to work out problems.

As for me, I'd call myself a late bloomer. I didn't date much in high school, though I had lots of male friends. One of those friendships turned into a rocky romance that continued on through the first year of college. Carl and I started out sharing a strong faith together, and having lots of fun. But college changed him, and he abandoned faith—and me along with it.

After having been "burned" badly, I shied away from romance for a while, keeping relationships with guys on a friendship level only. Looking back now, I see that I grew a lot through those friendships—but I still would have been better off if I had risked loving again a little sooner. Nonetheless, lessons learned during those non-romantic years have helped me to build a marriage that continues to bring deep satisfaction after ten years.

Dating can lead to lasting, satisfying love—or it can lead to misery, depending on the choices we make. This book is a guide to those choices. It's based on the real lives of people who have taken the available routes to love, and can tell you which ones lead to fulfillment—and which lead to danger. They can point out the potholes and rocky places, and advise you on the best techniques for survival.

1. *The Dream of Perfect Love*

We all dream of a special person. When we start to go out with someone, we wonder deep inside, *Is this the one? Is this the relationship that's going to turn into Something Special?*

In our hearts we carry an outline of that loving Special Relationship. It's an ideal that we're looking for, longing for.

When I asked students from all around the country what their ideal relationship would look like, the answers came readily. Before you read on, take a minute to answer the question for yourself. What would the ideal relationship be like for you? What kind of person would you be with? What would the two of you talk about? What would you do together? How would that Special Someone treat you? (If you're keeping a journal, you can write out your answers.)

> I would be with someone who knows that I'm not perfect and wants to spend time with me despite that. He would be able to talk with me about everyday things like school, basketball, friends, and our relationship, how we're feeling, what our needs are. He would treat me with respect but also as a strong individual with my own personality. Gentleness and romance are important too. Kissing's great, but there are times I would just like to be held in his arms.
>
> —*Laurie, 15, New York*

> The ideal relationship will be built on a firm foundation of trust. Both people would be able and willing to share feelings, needs, etc. Hopefully, there would be some common interests. I would want to be with a person who is warm, sensitive, and caring, and someone committed to

Jesus. She would treat me like I was one of the greatest people on earth, and I would do the same to her.

—*Robert, 18, Colorado*

To me, the ideal relationship would involve much caring. He would do special things for me like giving me candy or flowers or just a sweet note. I would be with a guy who knew what he wanted and wasn't afraid to stand up for what he believed in. We would talk about everything in life—our joys, problems, and different experiences.

—*Lois, 17, Iowa*

A person who was good-looking but more importantly has an outgoing, nice, caring personality. As we got to know each other better, we would be able to confide anything in each other. We would compromise on everything. No matter how bad a time was, we would still have fun because we were together.

—*Jonathan, 16, Wisconsin*

The relationship my fiancé and I have is nearly ideal. He has high intelligence (like I do), but we're talented in different areas, so we don't compete. We've never had a fight in four-plus years—we debate often, and we engage in open discussion of our feelings and desires, but we know how to compromise and be generous to avoid heated argument. We're open with our feelings, fears, goals, and needs. He often writes me notes and buys cards, flowers, and presents. Our best trait is our sense of humor. We can laugh about everything—even kissing.

—*Tami, 18, Virginia*

We would do a lot outside, like walks and hikes, picnics, camping, star-gazing, cloud watching, etc. We would have to be completely honest and open with each other, 100 percent, no matter what the situation. I wouldn't like it if I was the only thing in her life. She would be involved in something that she really enjoyed doing, something she really cared about.

We'd share mutual love—real love that isn't just there in good times but even when bad moods come up.
                                                    —*Rodney, 17, Alaska*

Trust. Openness. Mutual love, mutual respect. Shared values about the deepest matters of life: goals, dreams, faith in God. The ability to give, to understand, to help, but also to allow each other the space to be uniquely ourselves.

This is what I call the Dream. I think it's important to dream the Dream. Necessary even. I think God purposely made us capable of dreaming this Dream. I suspect Adam dreamed the Dream before God made Eve.

God made Adam, the first man, and then he brought to Adam the other creatures he had made. And the Bible says, "But for Adam no suitable helper was found" (Genesis 2:20). So God put Adam to sleep, and formed a woman out of a part of him. Catch the joy in Adam's words as he recognized the woman as the fulfillment of his Dream: "This is now bone of my bones and flesh of my flesh!" (Genesis 2:23). The Bible suggests that this Dream of intimacy is the basis for all marriages: "For this reason a man will leave his father and mother and be united to his wife, and they will become one flesh. The man and his wife were both naked, and they felt no shame" (Genesis 2:24–25).

IT'S A JOURNEY

When we begin to "date"—whatever form "getting together with the opposite sex" takes—we start a journey toward The Dream. It's not unlike the old childhood game of hunting for treasure. You have a treasure in mind—The Dream—and you have to find your way to this treasure.

While each person's path is unique, certain terrain has to be crossed. There's the usually-rocky road of starting out (how do you get a boyfriend or girlfriend?); the twisting, winding path of trying to understand what makes the opposite sex tick; the sunny meadow of a growing relationship; the hills encountered when the dream is in sight and

"Look, Mark, it's OK to be excited about your first date,
but don't you think you're getting a little carried away?"

you're getting serious; the thunder and lightning that must
be survived when problems arise; the valleys of breakups;
and the dry, waterless "desert" times when you're not in a
relationship at all.

AND IT'S A GAME

If dating is a journey toward a personal Dream, it's also
very much a game. There are certain rules. Some people are
more skillful at the game than others, and they seem to play
more often and with more partners.

In order to discern the rules of the dating game and sketch
a quick map of the possible terrain, I talked to several
groups of both high-school and college students from across
the country. I talked to groups of guys and girls, and groups
of just guys and just girls. What follows comes from hours of
discussions as we all tried to figure out how this institution
called "dating" (or simply "going out") works.

The Campus Life Guide

2. *Kids Talk About the Rules of the Game*

"I think he's interested, but I just don't know."

"I wonder if she really wants to go out with me?"

Those are the questions I started with in discussing "the rules of the game" with dozens of kids.

How do you know if the other person wants to go out? Well, there are the little signs . . .

Alex: If a girl doesn't show signs that she's interested in a guy, then the guy is most likely not going to ask her out. Guys don't want rejection.

Jenny: I think signs are really important. It's too blunt to just go up to a guy and say, "Do you want to go out?" It's much more comfortable if you're subtle about it.

Julia: I never did get the knack of this thing of "showing signs." I guess it just seems so fake to me or something. Or I think I'm sending out signals, and they're either ignored or misread. I just don't seem to get it.

Jenny L.: The same signals that tell me a guy is interested in me are what I try to send out: lots of eye contact, laughing, smiling, little things like that.

Alex: Flirting a little.

Shane: There can be problems with flirting. I have a couple of friends who flirt with me a lot, but they flirt with everybody. That's just the way they are. It'd be easy to misread those signs.

Sarah: I don't know what guys think about a girl who is a total flirt, but a lot of my friends, myself included, are afraid to show signs because we don't want to be seen as that kind of girl.

Jessi: Guys do misunderstand the signs sometimes. A girl who is simply trying to be friendly to a guy can be seen as liking him.

Good point. What if the guy reads the signals wrong? Bad news. Letdowns. What do you do?

Debbie: It would put a girl's mind at ease if the guy would say something like, "Let's go out once and just be friends." Keeping the friendship side up-front in those initial stages would help keep the girl from feeling like she is leading him on if she goes out with him.

Kevin: On our campus, you go out a couple of times, and you're a couple. There's a lot of gossip—"Did you hear that Rudy is going out with Debbie?" kind of thing, and it scares guys off from asking girls out, because it's automatically more serious than you might want it to be.

Jenny: I always think it's best to be friends first. If you decide you want to make it more than that later, that's OK. But starting off with a good friendship, instead of looking for romance, is best.

Mike: I think dating friends is tricky. If the dating relationship doesn't work out, then you didn't just have a few lousy dates—you have lost a friend-ship.

"LOOK! I DID NOT STAND YOU UP ON THE MOST IMPORTANT DATE OF OUR LIVES LAST NIGHT, NOR IS MY CAVALIER ATTITUDE JEAPORDIZING THE STABILITY OF OUR RELATIONSHIP... GIRL, I DON'T EVEN KNOW WHO YOU ARE!"

Alex: I disagree. If it's a good friendship, it will usually fall back onto that friendship.

Jessi: You have to be careful, though. Everybody has different ideas about friendship. You have to talk it out and decide what "friend" really means to each of you.

Talk. Good word, talk. It's great to get things out. Up-front. Honest. Yet opening up isn't easy. Sometimes it seems impossible.

Libby: In my relationships I've always had to be the one to initiate a discussion on what our relationship was all about. It would be refreshing for once to have the guy initiate it.

Shane: Guys don't want to say anything because they think that if they get sensitive it wrecks their macho image.

Libby: I don't like it when a guy is afraid to express his own opinions. You ask him a simple question like, "Did you like the movie?" and he just says, "I don't know." It's like he's always afraid of saying something wrong, and if he does he just knows I won't like him.

Jenny: Guys should try to talk more. Maybe girls have to help them. One way a girl could help a guy talk is by letting him know that she's very interested in what he has to say.

Libby: There's the other side to that too. Another thing that turns me off is when a guy tries too hard. Like always trying to be around me or calling me on the phone a lot—it suffocates me.

Trying too hard. That's a problem—and a real turnoff. There are other problems, other turnoffs.

Jessi: I don't like macho talk. Take the guy who thinks he has to talk about football all night.

Debbie: I don't really mind if a guy's macho as long as it doesn't go too far. If a guy thinks he's being macho by cutting somebody down in front of his friends, then I lose respect for him real fast.

Jeff: Lack of eye contact really turns me off. Sometimes when I talk to a girl, she just keeps on walking. I think, *What am I even talking to you for?*

Heather: What turns me off is obnoxious, immature behavior. There's a difference between fooling around and being obnoxious.

Jenny L.: Here's something that really gets to me. You're talking with this guy and his ideas are real interesting—he seems very thoughtful and sensitive. You think he's the greatest. Then the next time you see him with his friends, he's a totally different person. A real show-off.

Andrew: What turns me off is when girls are too materialistic, too concerned with what they're wearing. Girls who expect me to spend lots of money on them.

Sure—we don't like those who concentrate only on "outward stuff." But when it comes right down to it—in all honesty— aren't looks a big reason a guy and a girl get to know each other?

Jessi: Some kind of physical attraction is essential. But the main attraction should be who you are—your personality.

Gregg: Looks get you the date. Personality keeps a person coming back for more.

Sarah: If you're in a room with a person whose pant legs hit him at midcalf and he's wiping his nose on his hand, that appearance speaks for him. I look for somebody that's clean cut. I mean he doesn't necessarily have to be the most handsome guy in the world, but he has to care about how he looks.

Alex: But it can all go too far. A lot of girls spend too much time worrying about their appearance. A guy takes maybe 15 minutes in the morning to get ready. Girls take more like 45 minutes to an hour and a half. Guys have two or three pairs of shoes max, and girls have between 12 and 20.

Sarah: How many guys, if they were put in a room with girls who spend 10 minutes in front of the mirror, would ask those girls out? Those are the girls you don't look at twice. You don't appreciate us as people.

Alex: There's appropriate grooming and then there are extremes.

Jenny L.: But did you say the extremes are 45 minutes? I mean, you have short hair, you don't wear makeup. It takes a little time for that sort of thing.

Kerri: I asked a guy I know if he had a choice between going out with a totally gorgeous girl who didn't have a brain in her head and an ugly girl with whom he could get along great, he said, "Gorgeous with no brain." I couldn't believe it!

Jenny L.: I'd like to add something besides appearance that really attracts me to a guy. I like him to have a positive attitude. A guy who can find something good out of a bad situation impresses me. And along with that, I like a guy with a good sense of humor.

Shane: Yeah, there's this one girl at my school who's very nice looking. But she always puts herself down.

Nice, clean appearance: Check (with some argument over mirror time). Upbeat attitudes: Check. Friends: Check? Do friends play a part in who you do (or don't) date? Should they?

Mike: Say I went out with a girl and a friend of mine said, "You know, I really don't like her." If I thought he was wrong, I wouldn't worry about what he had to say.

Jenny: I think that's good in theory. But most of the time that doesn't happen. If a girl's friends say something bad about the guy she's going out with, it's definitely going to influence her—no matter how hard she tries not to let it. You know your friends usually come first.

And sometimes your best friend can see things about the guy that you can't see.

Gary: Yes, sometimes it's nice to be able to see your relationship from another point of view. I didn't see something in a relationship that my sister warned me about, and I got hurt.

Sarah: I wouldn't take it into consideration if my friends thought the guy was ugly or something like that. If you find a person attractive, it shouldn't matter what others think. But they might have some good points about character flaws.

OK. Our friends do know us—maybe better than we know ourselves at times. But sometimes our friends offer advice based on something else. Call it status. Call it popularity.

Sonja: A lot of times you don't even consider dating somebody from a different group, even if you find him attractive. A guy from a different group or clique than your own is just written off.

Kerri: It's easier to go out with someone from a different school than from a different group in your own school.

Jenny: I know girls who go out with guys just for appearance's sake. Even if they don't like these guys, they'll date them just because their friends think they're cool, popular, or good-looking. That happens a lot.

Libby: But remember: You are the one who has to make the decision; you are the one who has to be happy. Sometimes you accept the suggestions and advice from a friend and other times you say, "Thanks, but no thanks."

There you have it. Some of the issues surrounding the game of relating to the opposite sex. Of course, we've only skimmed the surface of these issues. Let's delve a little deeper.

3. *Taking the Plunge*

It's all well and good to talk about "showing signs" and "sending out signals." Often this works. The person you're interested in picks up on the subtle hints and sends signals back, and pretty soon you're together.

But lots of times the person you want to go out with doesn't pick up on the signals. What do you do if you're one of the two people below?

• *Recently I started praying for a Christian boyfriend.* Not too long after that, Scott came and sat next to me at the table in art class. I have always known that he is a nice guy, but I never really knew him. Scott talked with me about all kinds of things. That happened a few days ago, and ever since then he has sat next to me in art. We always talk to each other a lot.

I have really grown to love him. He is so kind, so friendly, and has such good Christian morals. I am pretty sure that he likes me, too, but maybe just as a friend. My problem is that I would like to go out with him, but I don't know how to get a boyfriend/girlfriend relationship started. He either is too shy to ask me out, or has never thought about it, or doesn't want to go out with me. What can I do to get something going between us?

• *I am 15 years old and have never had a girlfriend.* There is one particular girl in my church who, I think, likes me. I'll call her Jane.

We have gone on several church outings together and she shows her affection for me by flirting. If this is a sign of love,

I am determined to ask her out. She is 18 years old, and just an all-around great girl.

I have two problems. The first is another guy, Jack. Jack is what you would call a stud. He's your average tall, dark and handsome male. Every moment he's around me, he seems to attract all the attention, especially from Jane. I feel Jane is being stolen from me.

My second problem is my own lack of courage. If Jane were ever alone with me in a room, it would be the perfect opportunity to ask her out. Trouble is, I'm not at all experienced in this; I don't think I have the courage to ask her out.

STUCK ON THE BANK?

When you strike out on the path to learning how to love, it's as if you're immediately faced with a lake. It's not a huge lake, nor a deep one. But it's there, nevertheless, and the only way to move ahead is to take the plunge.

Some people stall in front of this lake for a good long time. They keep putting off risking that initial plunge. If they're male, they may dream up a hundred reasons why they can't ask that special girl out. If they're female, they may rationalize that they can't stand flirting, or that it's "unfeminine" to initiate a relationship with a guy.

In the end, the only thing to do is take the plunge. The cold water may shock at first, but soon you'll find yourself swimming and, if not enjoying yourself exactly, at least getting across the first obstacle. For a guy this means, by whatever means possible, plucking up the courage to ask a girl out.

Here's how one guy sets himself up psychologically for possible rejection: "I adopt an 'I don't care' mindset. I ask someone out thinking we can just have fun together, and if something comes of it, fine. If not, no sweat. I try not to let my imagination run away with me, imagining what a great relationship we'll have, that she'll think I'm wonderful and love me to death, etc. I try to keep the approach light and casual the first time or two."

Another guy advises, "Once you've made up your mind that you're going to ask a girl out you should do it that night or that day in school rather than waiting three weeks to get up the courage. Relax and be yourself and realize your priorities, which means that the date is not one of your highest ones."

Initiating a relationship is a little trickier for a female. In some parts of the country, it's unthinkable for a girl to take the initiative with a guy. She's just supposed to wait until a guy picks up on the signals she sends out. If he lacks confidence, or doesn't quite know how to interpret signals, the girl is stuck. ("Guys can be pretty dense," two guys told me. "A girl shouldn't depend too much on subtle hints.")

There is something to be said for tradition, and one 16-year-old guy says it well: "I'm in favor of tradition basically because it gives some guidelines. Once you've been dating for a while some of this can change, but for the first couple of dates the guy should do the asking and paying to (1) show the girl where he stands, (2) leave that as the one pressure for him to conquer, (3) give the girl respect so that 4) her only pressure is to end it if she isn't having fun. In this way if a guy asks a girl out and then doesn't really enjoy himself, he can end the dates on that date and the girl can do the same. But if they both enjoy themselves, they won't be worried about who is going to ask whom."

Girls worry about "undermining a guy's masculinity" by asking him out first. However, I've found that most guys like the idea.

So if you're female, you do have some options. Option Number One: You can ask him out. This works best if you're in an area where this is somewhat acceptable, and if you are prepared for possible rejection. Here's one girl's happy experience:

JOHN FINALLY GETS UP THE
NERVE TO CALL LAURA.

The Campus Life Guide

I spent much of my winter break from college gathering the courage and making plans to ask out my friend Derrick, a sweet, very quiet high-school senior with whom I worked at a restaurant during three and a half years during high school. It was embarrassing. It was frightening. I drove two hours home from college, planning to ask him face-to-face if he'd like to go out the following weekend. As it ended up I chickened out and asked him on the phone instead, which I could have done without the long drive home!

But it wasn't important, because he said yes! I paid, because I had asked, and I was very glad when he calmly accepted the news that it was my treat (pizza and movie) rather than argue because "the guy should pay." It was pretty fun! He's very shy and I hadn't seen him since last summer, but in about ten minutes he was talking and being the friend I had come to know at the restaurant. It was well worth the risk of asking him out! But now it's his turn if there's another move to be made.

Of course, there's no guarantee that the guy will say yes. If you are rejected, it can help you understand better how guys feel when they take ego in hand to ask out a girl. You learn to empathize, and you might even learn how to make yourself more approachable to guys.

Option Number Two: You can invite him to do something in a group, such as a fancy dinner party at your home, or a social function. You can call him to ask about homework, or just to talk. This is more subtle, but it often works. At least it lets him know you're interested in him while giving him the opening to later make a "first official move."

Option Number Three: You can write him a letter or send him a message through a friend that you really like him and wish you could go out together. This leaves the initiative to him, though it is clear that you are really the one making the moves. Some girls depend on friends a lot to test the waters. Caution: If you send a letter or card, keep it on the light side while not skirting around the point. You don't want to tell a guy you're madly in love with him, but that you do think he's interesting and you'd like to get to know him better.

Option Number Four: You can continue being friendly and hope he gets the idea. However, remember that, as one girl said, "They don't tend to catch on." What seems like a blatant hint to you may be mere friendliness to him. On the other hand, some guys are turned off by excessive flirting. The trick is to find ways to get into conversations with a guy, to show that you are interested in him by treating him a little more specially than he sees you treating other guys.

4. *Jump-Starting a Conversation*

Just how do you go from eye contact to getting a date? Most often it starts with conversation. You want to get to know the other person, be your most interesting and fun self, and underscore your interest—lightly. But finding the first words can be a trial. Jonathan and Marianne Butler approach the subject. Lightly.

Jonathan: What's your sign?

Marianne: No, no. That's no way to start a conversation.

J: OK. It's hackneyed, stupid, and irrelevant, but it could be worse.

M: Yeah, you could ask for her sign and she could say, "Equestrian Crossing," or some such. People used to ask half seriously about your horoscope, but I suspect you can't learn much from a system that places Sandy Duncan and Adolf Hitler under the same sign.

J: I'll tell them what you and I do at parties.

M: Whisper it to me first. OK, sure, tell them.

J: After I've been circulating for a while, I walk up to her like I've never seen her before.

M: He walks up like he's Clint Eastwood and doesn't see me at all!

J: No, I try to put a move on her.

31

M: Let me tell you what he does. He glides up to me like he's James Bond, and he distorts his mouth into a leering sneer, and he lifts an eyebrow and enlarges one eye like he's wearing a monocle, and he says (after clearing his throat), "Are you a model or something?"

J: It's not that bad.

M: Yeah, yeah. Every time he takes on the same look and says the same thing, "Are you a model or something?" It would be better to say, "Do you have any jumper cables?" And whether I said yes or no, you'd say, "It's OK: I don't need any. I just think it's good to have jumper cables."

J: That's a better opening line than "Are you a model or something?"

M: A lot better.

J: What about using physical props to get things going? My dad asks, "Have I given you my card?" Then he pulls out a professional-style business card with nothing but "MY CARD" formally printed on it.

M: He's done that to me. That's funny. And it's a good opening, because after the chuckle it can lead to an extended discussion along the same lines. He can tell the person what he actually does for a living, or he can ask, "What do you do?"

J: That's the tough part in a conversation: Getting the "engine" running so it stays running long enough to get warm and run on its own.

    You're at a party with hors d'oeuvres in one hand, and you small talk one person and the thing dies. So you small talk someone else and that dies. And before you know it there's nobody left. You've killed the evening. So you hang around the guacamole dip to appear busy. How do you get a conversation going and keep it going?

M: It probably takes luck. Certainly personal chemistry.

J: Hey, baby, you're talking my forte; I majored in chemistry.

M: See, there you go again with your macho James Bond character. Rule number one is to relax and be yourself!

J: "Relax!" you say. That's like the advice from a Doberman owner who says, "The dog won't bite if you stay calm." It's easier said than done. In a social situation you feel tense and awkward. You're staring at a taut, razor-faced Doberman with bared teeth, and someone says, "Relax! That dog is a lovable house pet." How do you relax?

M: You slowly exhale. You smile. And you say something like "Was that your Porsche I just hit in the parking lot?" or "You know, you look an awful lot like Bruce Springsteen." You're never completely relaxed in these first encounters. You're always a little nervous. You see those experienced Hollywood actors who tell Johnny Carson on the "Tonight Show" that they feel nervous . . .

J: Do you think I look anything like Bruce Springsteen?

M: Nervousness is not necessarily a bad thing, unless you're straitjacketed by it. If you're not a little hyped before meeting someone, you'll probably be a bore. What you want to do is translate those nerves into social energy.

J: But what do you think?

M: About what?

J: About me and Springsteen.

M: I think you look more like Springsteen than you do Cyndi Lauper.

J: The trouble with physical appearance is that it means everything when you're getting to know someone.

M: Well, looks mean more when you first meet someone than at any other time.

J: Life isn't fair.

M: No, but you don't have to look like a movie star to look good. A little pizzazz goes a long way; warmth, charm, and a sparkly smile make more of an impact than a lifeless mannequin—however gorgeous.

J: Like those people we saw in the candy store window that froze like mannequins.

M: Exactly. The main thing is to work with what you've got and minimize your physical flaws. Don't try to solve a weight problem by pouring yourself into some too-tight Calvins.

J: For me you find the ideal combination of looks and personality in people who didn't get a lot of attention for their appearance early in life. No early stardom. Then later when they turn out nice looking, they've already developed in all sorts of other interesting ways.

M: Like me?

J: Like you. You know, one thing you're good at in a conversation is listening. You really hear people when they talk, and you bounce off what they say to you. You don't just bide time while they talk and then monologue back at them.

M: Zzzzzzzzzzzzzz. Oh, I'm sorry. What did you say? No, that's very nice of you to say. There are people who can stay alert only when they're talking. Or there are the people you talk to whose eyes glaze over because they've lost interest. Or their faces brighten in the middle of your sentence because they've thought of something to say and they can hardly wait until you finish so they can talk.

J: Or there are the people who always seem to respond to you with "That's nothing! You should have seen what happened to me."

M: The important thing in creating comfortable conversation is to make the other person feel good, feel supported, and not to show off yourself. You want to extend friendship. You want them to shine.

J: Yeah.

M: Size up people and tailor your conversation to them. Ask the unexpected questions to get at them as real people. "Do you keep a journal? What are you going to write about this party?" or "Do you walk in your sleep?" and if they say yes, you can ask, "Do you think that's a sign of deep neurosis?" Or if they say, "How should I know, I'm asleep then" you can say good-naturedly, "A real smart aleck, aren't you?"

J: I had a fellow talk to me once rather intensely about whether a person's name determined his identity. Like what difference does it make to a guy's personality if his name is Francis instead of John?

M: Like Johnny Cash's "Boy Named Sue." Another thing about conversation is to show your own vulnerability. Everyone wants to be in control—the big star making the grand entrance in a movie. We never see, of course, all the outtakes they had to film before they finally got the scene right.

J: We ordinary people live the outtakes.

M: Yes. And it's so much easier and more comfortable to admit it. To say to the person next to you, "I never know quite how to act at a big party like this. What am I supposed to be doing now?" That gives someone a chance to help you out.

J: You know, I've been thinking.

M: What?

J: You do look like a model.

M: Well, if you did your hair differently, I think you'd look like Bruce Springsteen.

The Campus Life Guide

5. What Girls and Guys Really Want

We start our journey toward the Dream with a set of assumptions about the opposite sex. Sometimes the assumptions are based on experience. Often, however, our assumptions are based more on "what's in the air." "What's in the air" comes from television, ads, and movies, as well as what we observe our friends doing.

I asked hundreds of teenagers to give me their true feelings about what they think the opposite sex looks for in them, and what they really look for in the opposite sex.

Before you read on, you might want to gather your own thoughts on the subject. Reorder the following list of characteristics in order of their importance to you. The most important characteristic will be number one, the next important number two, and so on. (If a quality isn't important to you at all, don't even list it.)

athletic ability
attractive clothes
conversational ability
dependability
flirtatious nature
good grooming
good looks
good reputation
honesty
intelligence
manners and politeness

money
romantic nature
self-confidence
sense of humor
success orientation
warmth and sensitivity

Now, from the same list, rank what you think people from the opposite sex look for in you.

Remember, no one has to look at these lists but you, so be honest!

Are there differences in the two lists? There were in the *Campus Life* survey. Here are the answers we received. They throw light on some very interesting misunderstandings guys and girls have about one another.

WHAT GUYS REALLY WANT ... ─────────────

Here's the breakdown of what girls think is important to guys:

1. good grooming
2. good looks
3. honesty
4. warmth and sensitivity
5. dependability
6. conversational ability
7. sense of humor
8. good reputation
9. self-confidence
10. attractive clothes
11. flirtatious nature
12. romantic nature
13. manners and politeness
14. intelligence
15. success orientation
16. money
17. athletic ability

The Campus Life Guide

Now let's look at what guys say really is most important:

1. honesty
2. warmth and sensitivity
3. dependability
4. conversational ability
5. sense of humor
6. self-confidence
7. good grooming
8. manners and politeness
9. intelligence
10. good looks
11. good reputation
12. romantic nature
13. success orientation
11. attractive clothes
15. athletic ability
16. flirtatious nature
17. money

LOOKS NUMBER 10? BE REAL, GUYS! _____

I can hear female readers saying, "Come on, be real, guys! You're telling me that 'good looks' are more than halfway down your list?"

In most of the discussion groups I was involved in, guys admitted that they look for "looks and personality." Since there are many factors involved in "personality," I broke that up into qualities like "sense of humor" and "self-confidence."

But we can also say that "good looks" are made up of several things: "good grooming" (which both guys and girls picked as slightly more important than what you're born with), and even perhaps "warmth and sensitivity." The guys I talked with don't deny looks are important. One guy summed it up well when he said, "Looks may not keep the date, but they get the first one."

Yet many of the young men I talked to insisted that their

definition of "good looks" is broader than many girls might think. One college guy told me, "A girl may not think she's very pretty, but then I see her smile in a certain way and that smile wins me over. She has become beautiful to me." His words jive with a survey conducted by *Teen* magazine, which found that the number-one thing guys are attracted to is a friendly, open smile. Even before a pretty face.

Apparently guys don't pay as much attention to a girl's clothes as girls think they do. While girls think clothes are not too important, it's safe to say that guys think clothes aren't important at all. I suspect that guys look at the total package, summed up in "good looks," and don't pay all that much attention to a girl's clothes. Girls, on the other hand, are more aware of clothes, on themselves and on other females.

I think these findings are important because they go against the grain of our society. Girls are urged to try to become beauty queens, and to assume that unless they are, guys won't be interested. But if attractiveness is made up of two parts we can improve (grooming and the warmth we radiate) with only one part we can't change (what we're actually born with), there's hope for all of us.

We'll say more about looks in a minute, when we find out how important looks are to girls.

WHAT ABOUT REPUTATION?

Another thing that strikes me about these two lists is that girls thought a good reputation is more important to guys than guys actually say it is. Perhaps this is because guys know that, as one high-school senior admitted, "You can't believe what most of the guys say about girls. Guys lie a lot." Why? "So they can have a reputation and look cool."

The old "double standard" still exists. It's "cool" for a guy to "have a reputation," but it's bad for a girl to "have a reputation."

In the wake of the so-called "sexual revolution," this hasn't really changed all that much. In your parents' day, "nice girls" had good reputations and were the ones guys wanted to marry. What has probably changed since those days is the number of girls who agree that keeping a good reputation is important. When asked whether they agreed with the statement, "I think keeping a good reputation is important," 65 percent of the girls strongly agreed. Only 57 percent of the guys agreed—a little over half. Most of these respondents would call themselves Christian.

We'll talk more about the sexual pressures both guys and girls feel in a later chapter. At this point it's enough to say that there's still a problem here. (As if you didn't know.)

AND DON'T UNDERESTIMATE ...

Girls underestimated a few things. Maybe girls take it for granted, but "niceness" or the downright thoughtfulness implied in the idea of "manners and politeness" was rated "very important" by 40 percent of the guys, and came out eighth (not 13th) on the list of attractive qualities.

Then there's dependability. To 71 percent of the guys, this was very important; girls ranked it lower.

And what about intelligence? Girls ranked it 14th, with only 8 percent saying they think intelligence in a girl is very important. But guys ranked it 9th. Again, perhaps the girls were coming from the old stereotype that "guys don't like girls with brains." Intelligence may not be tops on the list for guys, but it's not on the bottom either.

AND THE GUYS THOUGHT ...

Now let's see what guys think girls look for:

1. Honesty
2. Warmth and sensitivity
3. Good grooming
4. Dependability
5. Good looks
6. Self-confidence
7. Sense of humor

8. Conversational ability
9. Romantic nature
10. Good reputation
11. Manners and politeness
12. Success orientation
13. Athletic ability
14. Attractive clothes
15. Money
16. Intelligence
17. Flirtatious nature

AND HERE'S WHAT GIRLS SAY THEY REALLY LOOK FOR . . .

1. Honesty
2. Warmth and sensitivity
3. Dependability
4. Manners and politeness
5. Conversational ability
6. Good grooming
7. Sense of humor
8. Self-confidence
9. Good reputation
10. Intelligence
11. Romantic nature
12. Success orientation
13. Good looks
14. Attractive clothes
15. Athletic ability
16. A flirtatious nature
17. Money

MIND YOUR MANNERS, GUYS!

The most glaring difference between these two lists is how much the guys underestimated the importance of "manners and politeness." Girls ranked it fourth, guys eleventh! Guys, you have to understand that girls want to feel cared for. Special. Thoughtfulness and downright courteous behavior translate into caring. It's more important than giving her gifts and flowers (romantic nature ranked 11, not 9 as you guys thought), more important than your looks, grooming, ability to tell jokes or to toss a football.

I might add that guys who are polite and considerate also win points with a girl's folks—something to keep in mind if you want to see a girl again after you meet her parents.

Then there's dependability. Girls think it's very important—81 percent of them said so. Only 58 percent of the guys thought dependability is very important to girls, though it was the number-three trait they looked for in girls. In some ways, we're not so different after all.

Perhaps the word "sensitivity" could use a bit of definition here. Another word could be "vulnerability." Girls respond when guys talk about their feelings with them, when they're not afraid to show that they are human. The exact opposite of the "macho" man, who looks like he has it all together and doesn't need anyone.

Yet girls don't want their guys to be "wimps," either. One girl clarifies the difference between "sensitive" and "wimp": "The attractive kind of sensitivity is when a guy is aware of other people's needs and feelings. The wimpy kind of sensitivity is someone who's trying to be so sensitive, so nice, that he's not in control of the situation he's in, he's just trying to be Mr. Nice Guy." The kind of guy who will do anything just to please other people.

The "Mr. Nice Guy" syndrome is definitely not what girls mean by sensitivity. Rather, it's the kind of person who can be "real," even when "real" means feeling hurt or disgusted or angry or vulnerable or sad.

Once a male friend insisted to me that guys are really more sensitive than girls, but that they are afraid to show their feelings because of the reactions they get. Fair enough. Society doesn't allow men to cry. And guys rarely can show "weakness" or emotion in the presence of other guys. But in the security of a good relationship we can be free to be who we really are, to be open about whatever we're really going through. That's the kind of relationship girls want with their boyfriends.

BRAINS OVER BRAWN?

Girls also thought intelligence is much more important than athletic ability. To 30 percent of the girls who responded to the survey, intelligence was "very important," while only 5 percent said athletic ability was "very important." Like girls, guys underestimated how attractive intelligence can be.

And what about looks in general? While guys thought good looks were pretty important to girls (they would rank it number 5), girls claimed they were pretty low on the list (number 13).

SURPRISE, SURPRISE

Are you surprised by any of these findings? Were you shocked that good looks is consistently overrated by both guys and girls? Did it surprise you that intelligence is more important than either guys or girls thought it would be?

What strikes me are the differences between what guys and girls really want, and what they think people of the opposite sex look for in them. We end up conforming to some image of what the opposite sex wants, and then we're frustrated when our efforts don't work. Girls, under the mistaken notion that guys are attracted to nice clothes, spend hours and all their spare cash shopping, when in reality, clothes just aren't important to guys. A guy spends lots of energy trying to be "macho" and "strong," not realizing that his girlfriend is secretly hoping he'll someday "open up" and share how he really feels—about school, about his family life, about her.

Another thing that strikes me is how the "rules" of the dating game differ from what people really want. Think of the following "rules" that are part of what's "in the air" around us:

"The guy always has to ask out the girl."

"You should only go out with the best-looking person you can get."

"If a guy doesn't 'score' he's not quite a man."

"If a guy shows his feelings he's a wimp."

"If a girl is smart, she should hide it or it will turn guys off."

It's strange how we all play by the rules of the dating game, even though many of these rules lead us away from what we really want.

6. If I Could Change One Thing ...

"If you could change one thing about how guys and girls relate to each other, what would it be and why?" That was the question posed to hundreds of *Campus Life* readers. Their answers cut through the games we play and reveal what people are really looking for.

WHAT GIRLS WANT: COMMUNICATION

The overwhelming majority of girls mentioned "communication" as the first thing they would improve.

Improved communication means, as one girl put it, "talking openly about things rather than being so afraid of what each other will think." To others it means being straightforward rather than "dropping hints and everyone wondering where the others are coming from." This includes being able to talk openly about the relationship itself, and about feelings (which gets us back to the sensitivity girls look for in guys). Openness, as opposed to playing mind games. Honesty, as opposed to assuming or wondering until someone gets hurt. As 17-year-old Lisa from California said, "Guys and girls are afraid to say how they feel and so they go behind each other's back and do and say things that hurt."

And communication doesn't mean just talking; it means listening, too, and understanding the feelings behind the words.

Girls mentioned communication in relation to sex: they want to "communicate about more than sex," to get rid of pressure to have sex and "just get to know each other and have a good time." Girls don't see sex itself as a way of getting to know each other and having a good time. Talking, laughing together, being who you really are with each other build a relationship. Sex doesn't.

MORE THAN A "PIECE OF MEAT"

The second thing mentioned most often can be summed up in a word: respect. To be seen as a person, not as a status symbol or a sex object or a pleasure source. Laments one girl, "I just want a guy to like me for the person I am, not what I can give him." Or, as Rachel, a 17-year-old from New Mexico, put it, "I wish guys understood that girls are not 'pieces of meat' and don't appreciate being used."

"I would want to change the concept of 'getting all you can' from one another," said a 15-year-old from New York. And 17-year-old Debbie from Tennessee asks pointedly, "Without respect for someone, how can you love them? When I say respect I mean as a whole person, that person's values, beliefs, opinions, and body."

Girls are aware of the way guys talk about girls. "Guys are often known for lying," says Lorraine, a 15-year-old Texan. "Sometimes you don't know what to believe."

The emphasis on sex, so prevalent in our society and among guys, is something most girls would change. "Too many people think a date or a relationship has to have some kind of sex. It doesn't! Sex is not what makes a relationship," Susan, a high-school sophomore from Indiana, told me. Karen Joy, a junior from Nebraska, shared her disgust at an attitude she's picked up at her school: "That all girls, no matter what, are easy! I hate having to duck sexual conversations that are meant to degrade girls," she added.

Related to respect is how girls are treated in front of a guy's friends—when she's there and when she isn't. Some girls wonder what a guy will say to his friends. This doubt undermines trust in a relationship.

LOOK TO WHAT LASTS

Another girl brought up, "The emphasis that both guys and girls put on outward physical appearance, popularity, and outward personality—I'd change that. I'd like people to be able to look beyond all that to the things inside. I know a lot of girls who are so wonderful and sweet inside, but they never get asked out because maybe they're kind of plain, or quiet. Yet they have so much to offer from within."

Other things girls would like changed: that girls and guys would be able to be friends first; that there would be more freedom to date casually without getting serious so fast; that there would be more trust between guys and girls; that guys would work harder at relationships and take more responsibility for the relationship.

WHAT GUYS WANT: HONESTY

Guys didn't use the same word, *communication*, that girls did. Yet "openness and honesty" top their list of things they would change about male-female relationships. "I wish girls would be more open about their feelings without intimidating us guys," says one. Girls may want guys to be more open about their feelings, but guys think girls could be more straightforward about theirs—specifically, when they're interested in a guy. Says one 16-year-old guy: "It's hard to tell if someone likes you or is just being friendly—people aren't open enough." Because natural friendliness in a girl can be interpreted as a come-on by a guy (or vice versa), signals get crossed and hurt feelings result. It's probably inevitable, but it would happen a lot less frequently if we could muster the courage to be open and straightforward about what we feel.

Another top "would change" item for guys: they wish the whole dating game would somehow become more comfortable for them. They mention the social pressures to date. They mention fear of rejection. They wish guys and girls could just be friends with each other first. (Sound familiar, girls?)

A lot of these concerns add up to a desire for girls to take the initiative more. Guys' third-most-mentioned wish is that "girls would feel more comfortable about asking guys out." To the question, "How comfortable do you feel about the idea of a girl asking a guy out?" more guys than girls said, "I think it's a great idea." Of the guys who thought it would be great for girls to ask out guys, more were from rural towns than were from cities or suburbs. So if you're female and wondering if you should take the initiative with a guy you like, take into account where you live.

Other things guys would change: "that girls would take more responsibility in relationships"; an end to cliques and popularity games and stereotypes; more interest in the person rather than the way he's packaged (appearance); and more trust.

ALIKE, YET DIFFERENT

Sound familiar? The beauty and mystery of the whole dating/relating game is that we're really so alike, yet so different. Guys and girls really want the same things: openness, honesty, respect, trust, consideration. Guys and girls both battle the same tendencies: to use people for their own gratification, to play games, to hide behind fear.

You can't change the whole dating game; the rules will remain. But you can change how you play the game. And that could make all the difference in building relationships that are open, honest, comfortable, and marked by respect.

7. *If Guys Only Knew*

What do girls wish guys understood about them? Lots!

IF GUYS ONLY KNEW WHAT IT'S LIKE TO WAIT TO BE ASKED OUT

For girls, getting a guy to ask them out is a fine art. One that doesn't always work despite a girl's best efforts. The girls I talked to mentioned the signals they try to send out: complimenting guys, asking open-ended questions about a guy's interests, giving him "that special look," dropping hints to his best friend, "being nice and smiling a lot."

Some girls resort to trying to be what they think a guy will like. But that's a wrong move, said Jenny, a senior from Wisconsin. "If you start putting on different acts and saying, 'Maybe he'll like me if I'm more hyper' or 'Maybe he'll like me if I'm more quiet,' and then you end up getting together, you're going to be miserable trying to live up to who you think he thinks you are."

It's especially hard to be a senior girl. Libby related: "I was talking to a boy who was going to homecoming with a girl he had never met. His friend had a girlfriend who was going to bring another girl for him, and he was just so unhappy about it. I said, 'Well, Dave, why didn't you ask one of the senior girls?' He said, 'The only senior girls I would want to ask are you and Kerry,' and I said, 'Well, why didn't you ask?' He said, 'I'm really afraid of rejection.'"

IF GUYS ONLY KNEW HOW IT FEELS TO BE UNNOTICED _____

What does a girl do if the guy she likes ignores all those subtle signals she sends his way? "Cry," one girls says simply.

"Sometimes all you can do is talk to him and try to be his friend and hope he gets the hint," says another. "It's hard because you don't want to be too forward, which might turn a guy off."

"You can't help but take it as rejection," says another. "All I have to do is tell my friends I like someone and it will get to the guy in 10 minutes. So if nothing happens I know he doesn't like me back."

Girls know what it's like to feel rejection too.

If you're a girl: How do you feel about yourself when a guy ignores you? Lots of girls jump to the conclusion that there must be something wrong with them. The truth is, the guy might have his own problems. Or you just might not be his type. It doesn't mean there's something lacking in you. Try to be aware of the messages you're telling yourself if you face this kind of rejection. And use your own understanding of how rejection feels when some guy you don't particularly like wants to go out with you; be tactful in how you say no.

If you're a guy: Remember that girls know what rejection feels like, too. They feel rejected when they want to go out with you and you don't ask. Instead of just ignoring someone you know likes you, why not look for ways to include her in some casual group activities? And why not be up-front: "I don't really want to go out with you, but we can be friends." It's an old line, one that girls give guys when they don't want to go out. But sometimes it's the only honest answer. Do we really value honesty most of all, as we claim?

IF GUYS ONLY KNEW THAT IMAGE ISN'T EVERYTHING _____

"I wish guys understood that there is more to girls than their looks," says 17-year-old Tanya wistfully. "Me, I'm not gorgeous, and I wish guys would get to know me first before

"I'm afraid this will have to be our last date, Eddie... you're just a little too weird for me."

they cross me off their list." After a moment she adds, "I would rather be me than some dashingly beautiful lady that all the men fall all over. This way I know that when they love me, they love me for me and not for my looks."

Many other girls agreed. "I wish guys would realize that the girls who aren't the prettiest are often the most interesting," sighs one 15-year-old. "It hurts to know the guys only go for outward qualities," says another. And 16-year-old Shannon told me, "When guys get to know me, they like me. It's just getting past the fact that I'm not a supermodel, just 'cute.'"

Girls mentioned other barriers to relationships. Such as:

Popularity games. "If a popular guy asks out a girl who isn't part of the popular crowd (which rarely happens), his friends could pressure him about going out with her, and he could drop her even though he might really like her," says Jenny. (The girls admit the same thing happens when a popular girl goes out with a not-so-popular guy.) "And it seems like sometimes the people in cliques who date each other don't even like each other; it's just the image of the thing—Mr. and Ms. Perfect," she adds.

Stereotyping. Certain stereotypes prevail, and it's very hard to shake them. Says Sarah, "At our school, my friends are the kind of girls that get elected, let's say, for the prom committee, and then they have trouble finding a date for the prom. They are the kind of girls that are nice to everybody, but they are either too intimidating because they're smart, or they don't smoke or drink so the guys figure, 'Hey, I won't have any fun with her,' so sometimes they have a hard time finding a date."

Here are two common stereotypes: smart girls are no fun to be with; and Christians are a drag (because they have morals). About the first, 17-year-old Maria from Indiana says, "I wish guys would realize that I'm fun because I am intelligent, and it's known in my school that I have this brain mystique, which scares guys away. Or they think I can just be a friend, that I'm incapable of going out on a date."

And about being Christian, Becky, a junior in high school, speaks for others when she says, "Even though I am a Christian, I'm still a lot of fun. Although my idea of fun is a little different, I'm still exciting and ambitious." Another 16-year-old says simply, "I wish guys understood that I'm not a goody-goody, only a girl with morals."

Once you're stereotyped, it's very hard to escape. Says Libby, "If a girl has a reputation for being really smart, for instance, and she is sick of it and wants to change, she may be willing to do anything. So she goes out with a certain type of guy and maybe her image does change, but not always for the better."

IF GUYS ONLY KNEW HOW HARD IT IS TO TURN THEM DOWN

It may not seem so, but girls really don't like to turn a guy down for a date. Many girls have an inkling how hard it can be for a guy to get up the courage to ask a girl out; they know getting turned down smarts.

So how can a girl let a guy down gently? "It's best to be honest," says Jenny. "If you know you really don't like him, just say, 'No, because I just feel differently about you.' You have to fit the words to the individual situation. But you end up hurting him more if you lead him on."

But some girls think you should give any guy a try. "You don't really know if the guy will act differently when he's just with you. You might be judging him before you get to know him. I think you should go out on one date at least. Then it might not hurt so much, if you can say, 'We gave it a try and things didn't connect,'" says Jessi.

Girls admitted that, while openness is the ideal, they sometimes resort to excuses, hoping the guy will get the hint. Or they just make it real hard for the guy to ask in the first place. And while it's best to turn a guy down in person, some do it over the phone or (admittedly the coward's way out) through a friend.

8. *If Girls Only Knew*

If girls had their list of "pet peeves" about the dating game, so did guys.

IF GIRLS ONLY KNEW HOW TO LIKE US FOR WHO WE ARE

It's true: a guy can act a little crazy at times—especially when he's with his friends. The guy calls it fun; the girl calls it immature. And she sets out to do something about it.

That kind of fit-into-my-expectations attitude rubs guys the wrong way. "I really get mad when a girl tries to change a guy overnight," Tim told me. While the guys admitted that maybe they do need to do some changing—to be more open, learn to talk more, become a little less rowdy—they appreciate being accepted for who they are right now.

IF GIRLS ONLY KNEW WE'RE NOT READY TO GET SERIOUS

What's on your mind when you start going out with someone? Are you thinking, "Is this the perfect relationship—the one that will lead to marriage?"

The teenage guys I interviewed said that when they date they aren't out shopping for that potential mate. "I'm 16 years old," said Jeff. "I'm not thinking about marriage right now. I want to put more emphasis on having a good time. I don't even think about marriage at all."

Furthermore, the guys are leery about making dating a

trial period for future marriage. "Maybe that happens when you're dating in college, but not in high school," said Shane.

Such pressure rarely helps a relationship; instead, it keeps it from unfolding naturally. It's like forcing a bud to bloom.

If that's so, why go out at all? First, for meaningful friendship. "Dating a girl is developing a friendship that's maybe a little bit deeper than other friendships," Alex told me. Second, because going out with someone we're attracted to helps us learn how to handle these feelings.

For both guys and girls: Think about what pressures you experience concerning dating. Do the pressures come from within you? From your girlfriend or boyfriend? From other people? Do you give in to the pressures or go against them? How?

IF GIRLS ONLY KNEW GUYS HAVE FEELINGS TOO

"Guys have feelings too, and just because a guy is a guy doesn't mean he can't get hurt. Just be aware of that." Such are the words of one guy I talked to, and many, many other guys echoed his sentiments. Girls can be awfully cruel and cold, they told me. They give inane excuses when they don't want to go out with you. ("'I have to wash my hair that night,' one girl told me," said a guy. "What does she take me for, an idiot?")

I asked guys about being turned down. It's never easy, they told me. They know the lines girls give, and generally understand anything but an enthusiastic yes to be a rejection. "Not too many girls will totally blow you off. Ninety-nine percent of them will say, 'Let's just be friends,'" one guy explained. "Does that help?" I asked. "No," John replied, "it's just a cop out."

Is there any way a girl can make turning a guy down any easier for the guy? "Not really, it just has to wear off," the guys told me.

But the girl's attitude makes some difference. If she's sincere, the guys told me, if you can tell she's trying to be sensitive and honest, that helps. Obviously, we're back to the whole issue of honesty—one of the attributes guys most appreciate. This is one of the major reasons why.

I'D REALLY LIKE TO SEE "NIGHT OF THE PSYCHO SQUID" WITH YOU EARL, BUT...I...UH.. HAVE TO ORGANIZE MY SOCK DRAWER THAT NIGHT.

LORI TACTFULLY DECLINES EARL'S INVITATION.

Guys like to know where they stand with a girl. "I think guys like some response from the girls in terms of how they're feeling about you," one college guy told me. "If you ask a girl out the second time, and she does like you, she should give some specific signal. Like a thank-you note for a date you've been on, or some specific signal that cannot be misinterpreted. Guys tend to be more expressive. Just by asking her out four times I'm telling her how I feel."

Another guy agreed. "That's probably the number-one

thing I wish girls understood, because I always like to know where I stand. I don't like to plague a girl by asking her out five times just to find out on the sixth date that she really didn't want me to ask her out all those times." Guys appreciate clear signals. Again, honesty.

Another way girls are insensitive to guys is in talking about other guys in front of them, like the guy isn't even there. "You always hear about locker-room talk by the guys, but girls do it, too. In fact, sometimes I think girls will tend to do it even more than guys. I've sat with a group of girls who talk about this cute guy walking down the hall. That kind of hurts. I sit there and think, *Well, what about me?*"

Girls complain that guys won't open up. Guys counter, "We're afraid to. We know you girls talk about us, talk behind our backs. And if we break up, how do we know you won't say things about us because you're mad at us?"

If you're a girl: Think for a minute about times you may have hurt a guy. How many times have you made up dumb excuses about why you can't go out with someone? Try this: Each time a guy asks you out and you don't want to go out with him, take a minute to imagine it's you asking him out. If he didn't want to go out with you, what would be the best way to let you know that? Any guy is going to feel bad if you turn him down, but at least if you're honest, he can appreciate and accept that. Guys understand what the line, "I just want to be friends" means, but often it's the most honest way to respond.

Another thing, girls. Guys can't read your minds. One girl wrote, "I wish that guys knew when I was upset or hurt without having to tell them." Well, they don't, and it's unfair to expect them to. If we're upset about something, we have to tell them what. And if we had a good time on a date, we have to find some way to say so. Most guys just aren't trained to pick up on subtle body-language clues. (And face it: often even your best friend doesn't pick up on what you're really feeling.) Guys do understand clear words. If you had a nice time on a date, you can give him a big smile and say, "I had a really great time. Let's do it again sometime!" That's pretty clear.

IF GIRLS ONLY KNEW THAT VALUES ARE IMPORTANT TO GUYS _____

Girls may feel that guys only have sex on their minds. Well, the guys I heard from told me that sex pressures are unwelcome to them, too. They feel it from their friends, and from the general atmosphere. As a guy from Illinois put it, "People always ask you what you did last weekend, and the attitude is, what are you waiting for, are you just biding your time?" Jesse added, "There's a lot of pressure if you're a Christian, because you're a minority in a secular world. A non-Christian will ask you, 'Did you do such and such with your girlfriend?' and if you say no, their attitude toward you is that you're abnormal." Guys feel pulled in two different directions: On the one hand, they feel this tremendous pressure from friends (and their own hormones) to "prove you're a man" and "gain experience"; on the other, they may honestly want to respect a girl and hold to the Bible's standard of reserving sex for marriage alone.

One guy told me that he thought "about 60 percent of what you hear about guys' sexual exploits is lies." I asked why guys would lie so much. The answer: "So they can have a reputation and look cool."

I remember talking this over with my good friend Mark, when we were in high school. He hated the locker-room talk and refused to talk about what he did with his girlfriends. When asked, he would say matter-of-factly, "That's really none of your business." Most of the time, that was enough.

Occasionally, however, someone would be offended that Mark wouldn't play along with the games guys play. Rumors would start. I always admired Mark for hanging on to his values, even when it cost him a reputation for being a "stud" or "cool." And, I would add, it didn't seem to interfere with his finding girls to go out with.

Guys say that deep down they want "a good friend and

someone to honestly love, more than someone to hug and hold," to quote Matthew, a high-school sophomore from Michigan. And many guys are concerned that girls know they are "not like most guys these days." An 18-year-old named Andy from Colorado says, "I'm not dating just for show or to get anything from a girl. I just want to have fun and let her have fun too." A college sophomore complains about how "sex always seems to be a big-pressure issue."

There are Christian guys out there who are still virgins, girls: 72 percent of the guys who responded to the *Campus Life* survey were virgins (the average age of the respondents was 18). And 82 percent of the guys thought that it was important for a potential date to have the same spiritual values—much more important than that they be of the same race, age, denomination, or ethnic background. I'm sure this is higher than the "average population," because many of these guys were seriously committed to their faith. Still, it puts some perspective on the "everyone-is-doing-it" sense you get from listening to people talk.

In spite of the double standard, so-called "sexual equality" has brought changes. Guys told me they wanted to make sure a potential date's reputation was good because they didn't want sexual pressure from the girl to add to the pressures they already felt from other sources. And these guys gave me some advice to pass on to others.

To avoid compromise, Jeff said that you need to have your guidelines set before you start serious dating. "That way," he adds, "it's easier to say no to sex, drinking, and drugs." There was also a strong feeling that one's faith does have a place in dating relationships. "Physical attraction and personality are only part of it," said Alex. "You're still going to have to consider where the girl is in terms of spiritual maturity."

"Just don't give yourself the opportunity," said another guy. "Don't be alone in the house with her, for instance."

"There's always a way to get out of it," said Mark. "Like

you can say you have to go somewhere. Or you can make sure that most of the time you're around other people."

For both guys and girls: Many of us—if we're honest—are tempted in the heat of the moment. But there are some things you can do.

1. *Focus on the Dream.* When you're tempted, remind yourself of the kind of relationship you're moving toward, your Dream. Think through (ahead of time, and then remind yourself whenever necessary) these questions: "Would this activity move me toward or away from the Dream? Would this activity be respecting my own deepest-held values? Would this activity hurt the other person?"

2. *Set standards.* Sit down by yourself and write out how you feel about parties, drinking, drugs, kissing, petting, sex. Decide what you believe and allow that to carry over into your dating life. One guy advised, "Ask yourself, 'Would I do that in front of God?' If you can say yes to that question, then it's OK."

3. *Talk it over.* If you're going out with someone, discuss your values. As your relationship gets more serious, you will want to be sure you're both willing to honor the same standards.

4. *Plan ahead.* Think through how you would handle situations before they come up. For example: How would you respond to someone's pressuring you to talk about what you did on a date? How would you answer any of several "lines" ("If you loved me, you would", "Why is it wrong if we love each other?" etc.)?

5. *Look to God for help.* Temptations are ever-present, and they can be strong. Pray for the strength to hang on to the Dream. One young person gave me this bit of advice: Memorize 1 Corinthians 10:13: "No temptation has seized you except what is common to man. And God is faithful; he will not let you be tempted beyond what you can bear. But when you are tempted, he will also provide a way out so that you can stand up under it." When you're tempted, look for that way out.

Though incredibly shy, Dan finally figured out a way to ask Laurie Morganson to the prom.

IF GIRLS ONLY KNEW HOW HARD IT IS TO ALWAYS TAKE THE INITIATIVE

Taking the initiative is a role traditionally reserved for the male in our society. Lots of guys would like to see that changed. In fact, 88 percent of the guys said they would like a girl to ask them for a date, and 82 percent said they had been asked out by a girl. (This compares to 63 percent of the girls who said they would like to ask a guy out, and 59 percent who said they had done so.) When I brought up the subject of girls asking guys out, the typical response I got from guys was, "I'd love it!" Some would add, "It never happens, though." One guy told me wryly, "You can pretty much post a sign in front of girls saying, 'I will go out with you,' and they won't ask. They'll just wait for you to make the first move."

Sometimes, though, the girl's initiative plunges the guy into the whole dating game in the first place. More than one guy has told me what Mo, from Florida, said: "My very first date was when a girl asked me out."

Joe, a college sophomore from California, told me, "Most of my dates throughout high school came when a girl asked me out (we had what's known as Reverse Weekend where it is the girl's turn to ask out the guy). I have no problem with a girl asking a guy out for a date. I notice it happening more and more, and I think it's GREAT!" That's because Joe has a great deal of trouble feeling comfortable asking a girl out. "I have no problem standing in front of large audiences and giving speeches or presentations. I have no problem talking to people on a business level. I have no problem talking with small groups of fellow students on subjects that concern them. But when it comes to talking just to a girl, or asking one out, I become extremely shy and can't force myself to do it."

For a guy like Joe, tradition is uncomfortable. "Right now I am forcing myself to try to ask girls out on dates, but I must say that I have greatly enjoyed the dates where the girl has asked me out." Joe also doesn't mind if a girl makes the "first moves" physically. "That's how my first and third relationships were. My second one I got the guts to make the first move for the kiss, but I asked her first if I could do it. I should have just done it!"

Nothing's clear-cut anymore on this issue of roles, and who asks whom out, and even who pays. At any rate, it seems clear that most guys are willing to be approached. This makes for confusion (it's no longer so clear what the rules are for initiating a relationship), but it also means opportunities. No longer must a girl just wait. There is the distinct possibility that she can initiate a relationship, if she has the guts and can find the right approach.

9. Roles, Male and Female

When my boyfriend and I go out, he usually pays. He is the kind of man who believes a woman's place is in the home, not working, and the man puts the bread on the table. So hey, more power to him!

—*Brenda, 16, Pennsylvania*

I was raised in a home in which both parents worked. I think the wife is a better help to the family if she works, and the husband and wife can do household chores. I would rather see my wife have her own career goals. Women who have strong career goals seem to have more to offer all around. I'm more attracted to girls who are motivated by their own goals.

—*Andy, 19, Ohio*

I think the husband should get involved with the housework because when they got married they took a vow for better and for worse. Housekeeping is part of "worse"; it's something they should share.

—*Rachelle, 17, New Jersey*

As I talked with teenagers about roles, I mostly found this: Not too many people put a lot of thought into it. Most just figured it would work itself out as they went along.

If you're at the stage of casual dating, roles may not seem too important. But you're laying the groundwork for the kind of relationship that may deepen to something serious. If you are female and you go out with someone like Brenda's boyfriend, are you prepared to live with someone who wants to call all the shots for the rest of your life? If you're male,

"MAYBE I SHOULD EXPLAIN SOMETHING TO YOU ABOUT 'GOING DUTCH' ON A DATE."

The Campus Life Guide

would you rather have a wife like Andy describes, or would you prefer someone whose main ambition is to be a great wife and mother?

It's easy to have a naïve notion that "love will conquer all"—including differences over who is ultimately responsible for housekeeping or for paying the bills. Most people figure they can work these things out as they go along. And to some extent, they do. But there is one important condition: basic agreement on what a marriage is. Are you both sharing the same Dream? Is your Dream one of true partnership, or one of two people complementing each other? Either model can work, if both people fully agree to the terms, and if there is deep mutual respect.

If you're serious about laying the foundation for a solid relationship, you should probably think through which model you believe to be right for you. I'll give you some of the pros and cons of each, and some hints for how to pick up on subtle clues in a relationship that could spell trouble later on.

TRADITIONAL MODEL

You've probably seen this model in your own family or in a friend's family. It fits most of the stereotypes about male and female division of labor, and is viewed by some as the biblical norm. (Though in the Bible, the father is always commanded to participate fully in child-rearing, and the "ideal wife and mother" described in Proverbs 31 also seems to be a career woman.) In the traditional model, the man invests heavily in his career and is the chief breadwinner; the woman takes most of the day-to-day household and child-rearing responsibilities. She may or may not have a part-time job, but her focus is on the home.

My research revealed that more young men than young women subscribe to this model. Of those who plan to get married, 62 percent of the males said they would like their wives to work outside the home. But 79 percent of the young women said they planned to work outside the home.

It can be a set-up for disaster if there isn't basic agreement on this issue. I know an 18-year-old newlywed who has dreams of going to school and becoming a nurse, but her husband firmly believes that her place is in the home. Though she loves him, she is already chafing under his rigidity. A good friend of mine, who married at 17, found that this difference could not be reconciled. Though her husband finally "let" her attend college, he felt so threatened by her career goals that things went from bad to worse, and the marriage ended.

Most Christian couples who live the traditional model also believe the man is the head of the home. They point to such verses as Ephesians 5:23 ("the husband is the head of the wife, as Christ is the head of the church") and take this to mean that the man has the final authority. This subject is not one I can thoroughly discuss in this book; I will say that there are some fine biblical scholars who have carefully set forth a different viewpoint, one more in keeping with the second model, that of partnership. If this is an issue or a potential issue in your relationship, I suggest you take the time to do further study with your boyfriend or girlfriend so you both agree on your convictions.

Remember Andy, whom I quoted at the beginning of this chapter? He said he wants to marry a woman who has strong career goals of her own. But he also said, "God gave men the ability to make decisions. I think women make irrational decisions. I would expect my wife to give her input, and I would pray about the matter. No way should the woman be a servant. But she should submit to his decision even if it's wrong."

To me, Andy seems somewhat inconsistent. He wants someone who is strong enough to pursue her own career, someone who is definitely not a "servant" (meaning a patsy, I guess). At the same time, he believes all women make irrational decisions. So he would expect his wife to just "give input" while he makes the important decisions.

Andy's views should certainly be a clue to any strong-willed woman that there might be trouble ahead if she were to marry him.

There are advantages to the traditional approach if both people find that their gifts are well used in the spheres they choose. If a woman loves children and homemaking, she'd probably feel very fulfilled in a traditional relationship. A guy who is very career-minded and goal-oriented would also find this a good model. Under the traditional model, certain basic decisions are made; the couple doesn't have to continually negotiate who will do the grocery shopping this week or who will mow the lawn.

The weaknesses are these: Women often find that they need to be more in life than wives and mothers, even if they enjoy being wives and mothers. Husbands may become bored with wives who have nothing more to talk about than children. Communication is a challenge between two people whose everyday lives are very different. She is immersed in the consuming needs of children, he in the demands of his job. It takes work to keep their Dream alive.

PARTNERSHIP MODEL _____

In this model, the idea of equality is worked out on every practical level. Both people work at jobs they're committed to, and both are equally committed to home and family. Decision-making is mutual, with each person having equal input until a mutual decision is made. This will often call for compromise. There is a lot of negotiating to be done in this type of marriage, on everything from who will make tonight's meal to who will stay home today when the baby is sick.

Many young people hold this approach to the Dream, at least in theory. The advantages are obvious. Both parties have a share in all the responsibilities. Partnership binds the couple together. They have many things in common and can relate on many different levels. She has things to share from her job, just as he does. Both are involved in raising the children. A guiding principle for dividing chores can be:

Whoever does something best or minds doing it least, does that particular chore. So if the husband likes cooking, and she doesn't mind doing dishes, he can cook and she can do the dishes. Responsibilities are divvied up by individual strengths and preferences, rather than gender.

If sharing everything equally fits your Dream, this is the model you're looking at. You'll need someone who is as committed to both home and career as you are—and as willing to make the necessary trade-offs.

Because there are trade-offs. Both people may have to scale back on their career goals if a family is important. The constant negotiating may become wearisome. Both parties may feel pulled in different directions much of the time, and there is a constant juggling act going on. Studies show that women who work outside the home still do most of the housework. A man may say he believes in doing 50 percent of the housework, but that rarely happens. This leaves the woman feeling cheated and resentful, and the husband (if he's man enough) guilty for not living up to his end of the agreement.

COMMON SENSE, LOVE, RESPECT

I said that both models can work—or fail. Everything depends on attitude and commitment. The attitude must be one of respect. The commitment must be to a relationship that is growing, and to the good of the other person. How you choose to work out these principles doesn't matter all that much, provided you share the same basic values.

This doesn't start on the wedding day, but long before, in a dating relationship.

First of all, there must be freedom to be who you are— and an appreciation for who you are. Power must be evenly distributed. If the guy pays for the date, there isn't a sense that the girl then "owes" him anything.

Another hallmark: Each person shows respect and support for the other's goals. You have a sense that he or she wants whatever's best for you.

In 1 Corinthians 12, Paul talks about gifts and how one is to use them. Paul says, in a nutshell, that each person has gifts, and they are to be recognized and used for the good of the church. I believe this can also be applied to marriage or to dating relationships: Each person has certain "gifts" to bring to the relationship.

But after discussing gifts, Paul goes on to describe "a more excellent way" in chapter 13. He describes the kind of love that anyone can build a dream on:

"Love is patient, love is kind. It does not envy, it does not boast, it is not proud. It is not rude, it is not self-seeking, it is not easily angered, it keeps no record of wrongs. Love does not delight in evil but rejoices with the truth. It always protects, always trusts, always hopes, always perseveres."

In the next chapter, we'll look at some practical ways to cultivate this kind of relationship.

10. Friendship Plus: Nurturing the Dream

My ideal relationship would be a friendship first. With someone I can share spiritual things with. Someone I can share hardships with, someone that I can share trivial things with, and someone I can have fun with no matter where we are.

—*Daniel, 19, Arkansas*

It used to be that guys and girls were trained to see the opposite sex only in terms of romantic/sexual attraction. For some people, sadly, this is still true. But times are changing.

Nowadays, a lot of guys and girls are "just friends." Girls and guys need close friends of the opposite sex whom they can talk to about boyfriend or girlfriend problems. People they can just enjoy being with, without all the potential entanglements of romance. People they can go out with casually, without it being any big deal. One girl told me, "I can ask out a guy who's just a friend, but I could never ask someone I really liked out on a date."

Many people find "just friends" relaxed and comfortable. Combining friendship with romance is more complicated. There is liking (as in friendship) and there is Liking (as in romantic attraction). Sometimes liking develops into Liking. A friendship develops into Something More. Then there is awkwardness. Does the other person Like you too? Should you say anything? If you do, will it ruin the friendship? Should you go out with a good friend, or not?

Opinions are mixed on this issue. "There are some girls who are friends that I would consider dating, but I wouldn't want to jeopardize the relationship," a guy named Scott told me. "If I go out with somebody and then we break up and I lose the friendship, it's not worth dating the person." Most of the guys I talked to agreed with Scott: a friendship is more important than going out.

Girls also weren't sure going out with a friend is a good idea. Said one girl from Illinois, "My experience has been that when you go out with a friend and then break up, it's usually for a reason like they lied to you or something really went wrong. And if something like that happened then you are not going to want to be the guy's friend, either."

Then there's the sticky situation in which only one person comes to Like the other. Julie, a senior attending college in Illinois, shared her experiences: "I was friends with an older guy and he was trying to pursue the relationship. To me we were just friends. I had no romantic interest at all. It got so that instead of talking about it I just would avoid him at all costs. That wasn't right. I ended up hurting him.

"But in another instance a guy and I were driving somewhere after church and he told me he liked me a lot more than as a friend. He asked where our relationship was going. I had no clue that he was feeling this way. I thought we were just good friends. But it was good that he could tell me how he felt. We talked about it and we remained good friends."

Other people prefer to go out with a friend—and have had good experiences. Mo, a guy from Miami, Florida, said, "As long as you keep things in perspective and have a good dating relationship, then afterward you can come back to your friendship. That was what happened to me, anyway."

Hope, a friend of Mo's, pointed out that both Mo and his ex-girlfriend were pretty mature people. She added, "When people who are immature go out, they aren't always able to come back after they break up and say, 'Hey, let's keep our friendship.'"

One guy put it succinctly: "It depends on what happened

when you were going together. It depends on whether you hurt each other or not."

FRIENDSHIP PLUS _____

I think of good relationships—relationships that lead you toward the Dream—as a combination of two important ingredients.

The first is friendship. So many girls—guys too—talked about the importance of friendship. Friendship implies a level of comfortableness ("I can be myself with the person"); trust ("I can tell my friend everything and anything"); loyalty (you don't bad-mouth a true friend). You have fun with a friend. You learn from a friend. You are honest with a friend—no need to play games or cover up how you really feel. All those qualities we looked at in the previous chapter—honesty, communication, warmth and sensitivity, dependability—are attributes of healthy friendships.

But we go out with people for more than friendship. Dating is Friendship Plus. Friendship plus romance. Friendship plus sexual attraction. Friendship plus a deep longing to love and be loved by a special someone. Dating is what you do when you feel the stirrings of something calling you beyond friendship to the Dream.

Lots of people put down romantic love. They call it "mere infatuation." Perhaps this is because romantic love has been distorted by what's "in the air." Mostly, the sexual component has gotten blown out of proportion, so that sex is everywhere. It's on most television shows, in most movies. It's what advertising uses to sell products from toothpaste to cars.

The Plus side has also dominated the whole dating game; it's probably what makes it a game in the first place. Girls (and guys) complain about how people will only go out with good-looking (read, sexually attractive) people. Girls say guys want only one thing—sex. They get tired of having to deal with the whereabouts of a guy's hands on every date.

Guys feel bewildered by new and very powerful emotions that take over whenever they see an attractive female.

Some people react to all this. They say, in effect, "Let's ignore the Plus and just have friendship." One girl said, "I wish guys and girls could just be good friends with each other instead of having romantic interests." A guy named Jesse argued against the label "boyfriend/girlfriend." He explained: "I think girls are really smarter than guys when they try to keep things on a friendship basis. Because when you are on a friendship basis, and you have an argument, you work out your problems. You call the person back the next day, say 'I'm sorry' or whatever, and you're friends again. But if you and the person you're going out with have an argument, chances are you break up and then you never talk again."

From what I've heard, a majority of young people don't feel completely comfortable with the Plus side. George, presently a college sophomore from Ohio, met a girl at a weekend retreat while he was in high school. "This girl had just become a Christian. She had been abused when she was a child, and was kind of a mess emotionally. But it seemed like God was really making some changes in her life.

"But about five months into the relationship, we had sex. She pressured me into it. The relationship went on for two years before I could break it off. She was a compulsive liar, telling me she'd gotten pregnant and had an abortion, and other things. I began to drink and do drugs. Finally I ended the relationship, but I'm still working through the hurt. I still feel afraid of relationships; they have to start with friendship, and slowly grow as trust is built up."

It's clear that for George, Plus took over. Now he's very cautious about letting Plus enter any relationship. That may well make his journey toward the Dream a little longer than it would have been otherwise. But, as George himself will tell you, he's learned a lot about love. What it is. What it isn't. His picture of the Dream is definitely refined.

There's a very delicate balance to maintain. Most of us get

out of balance at some point, with more or less disastrous consequences. In my experience, and in my observations of couples who have good relationships, there is one essential ingredient to make the balance possible.

That balance is a shared faith.

FRIENDSHIP PLUS . . . GOD

"Why can't I go out with someone who isn't a Christian? It's not like I'm going to marry the person." I've heard this voiced a lot by young people. And I agree that common faith is most important when you're in a serious relationship. But I also think it's important in a Friendship Plus relationship.

The way to get to the Dream is to work on the Friendship and manage the Plus. You don't have to work at creating the Plus. The attraction is natural. You do have to work at managing all that sexual energy, or it can "burn" you. And the way to manage the Plus is to focus on the Friendship. Not exclusively, so we're pretending Plus doesn't exist (that's lying to ourselves). But carefully and persistently putting energy and attention on friendship. That's how to build your Dream.

Scott and Tiffany are three and a half years, and four grades, apart. When I interviewed them, they had been going out for over a year—thirteen months, to be exact. And they had known each other for a while before that. Other people in their youth group told me about this couple, about how they were a real example of a good relationship.

Scott: I had no intention of going out with Tiffany, really. There was such an age difference. When I first met Tiffany I was just trying to reach out and show her I'm her friend. We went out a lot in groups, and we slowly became closer and closer friends.

Tiffany: To tell you the truth, I had this crush on him for four months. Through that time God helped me learn patience, because I really liked Scott a lot, but God just told me that he was in control and that if he wanted me to go out with Scott then we would eventually. I just put that in his hands. Eventually Scott and I became good friends, then best friends, and then we just started going out.

Scott: Eventually I realized I did like her, but I was afraid to go out with her because of the age difference. To be honest, I was afraid of catching flack. But eventually I realized that that shouldn't be a factor. Also, our youth pastor talked to me, saying, "If you don't like her, tell her, because you keep coming over and giving her ideas."

So we started going out when I was a junior and she was 13. At first we kept it to ourselves. We didn't want to rush into anything. We still wanted to be good friends, and that was and still is the main purpose of the relationship. Friendship has to come first.

I played varsity football last year, for my senior year, and Tiffany was an eighth-grade cheerleader. I caught a lot of flack, especially from the other football players, because Tiffany was so young. But I would have caught flack even if we were the same age and went to the same school, because non-Christians don't see relationships the same way. It's like, once you date a while, they think you should be moving on to bigger and better things. But I decided to ignore the flack, because this was a special relationship. And because we were both Christians, our perspectives were different. We realized we had to totally depend upon God. We knew that if we tried to control the relationship, if we held back from God in this area, then it would fall apart and we'd get hurt. I care about Tiffany a lot and she cares about me a lot, but we both realize that Jesus must be Number One in our lives.

I imagine that, even if Scott and Tiffany decide their relationship needs to become less committed, the breakup will be friendly. The faith factor keeps them working on the Friendship and managing the Plus. Contrast the picture of their relationship with this one:

> I've been dating Mark for almost seven months. I am a struggling Christian. He has no religion. I plan to stay a virgin until I'm married, but he pressures me. In the beginning we talked everything out, set the rules. Mark says he loves and respects me but just can't help himself. I get tired of pushing him off, saying no. I get tired of trying to explain to him it's not because I don't love him. I find myself giving in because I don't want to lose him, because his wants become my wants.

This girl and her boyfriend don't share a common faith. Unlike Tiffany and Scott, who are both looking toward the same goal (obedience to God and his way) and depending on the same source of strength to keep Plus in check, this girl is torn. Torn between her faith and her feelings for her boyfriend. He probably honestly does want to respect his girlfriend and her standards. But his own desires are stronger. He has no faith to keep Plus in balance.

Without a strong faith, held in common, we end up having to make a choice. Do we follow our feelings (which can be very powerful) or do we follow our values? Put more simply, we end up having to choose between a boyfriend or girlfriend, and God.

I'm convinced that if you choose love over God, you're headed for disaster. Because romantic love is such a powerful emotion, it tends to take the place of God in your life. The relationship, for which you've sacrificed so much, becomes too important. You begin to ask it to give you a sense of meaning and identity and purpose, to take away any feeling of loneliness and make you feel perfectly safe and happy.

But no relationship with another imperfect human being can do this for you. A relationship can provide companionship. A relationship can offer the great gift of intimacy. But it will never provide meaning and purpose, security and identity. Those are spiritual needs met only by a personal relationship with God.

The kind of relationship we dream about grows out of a relationship with God. Love grows out of a full heart, not an empty, hungry one.

NURTURING LOVE

How do you do it? How can you have a positive, Friendship Plus relationship with another Christian? What, on a practical level, do you do and say? How do you act?

The first principle is to accept each other. That may sound odd, because you'd think that if you're willing to go out with each other, you must accept each other. But that's not necessarily so. I remember how nervous and uptight I often was on dates. I think I felt that way because the guy I was with felt so caught up in how he was coming off that it didn't occur to him to let me know he thought I was OK. I needed that accepting affirmation in order to relax and be myself. So did he.

You can't communicate an accepting attitude if you don't have one. As long as you're wishing your date looked better, talked better, had fewer hang-ups or more brains, you'll probably exert subtle pressures to make your date feel tense and unaccepted. (One guy confessed that the first thing his ex-girlfriend did after breaking up was go back to putting cream in her coffee. He'd been very evangelistic about black coffee.) If you can't accept and like your date just the way he or she is, don't go out together. You'll end up miserable, and your date will end up hurt.

Here's one girl's rather amusing experience:

"I had this immense crush on a guy who went to my

church when I was in seventh grade. He was then a senior. For over two years I would just look at him and daydream. I don't think he knew I existed except that his sister and cousin, who are my age, would always talk to him about me. It didn't do much good. He really intimidated me for a while. He was a gorgeous blond and dressed so fine that . . . oh my! And the thing that made it so terrible was that I was so homely (late bloomer with glasses) that my self-confidence was rock-bottom. So I just waited and prayed. Well, finally I made it to tenth grade, I had contacts by then, my confidence was built up, and I looked pretty good. I even started saying hi to the guy at church. One Sunday I invited him to go horseback riding with me—and he accepted! I was thrilled. So the next Saturday came up (I was about to have a cow by this time, just imagining how we'd be trailriding and suddenly he'd say out of the blue that he's always cared for me, blah, blah, blah), and we went horseback riding. Well, I found out that he was a human being. It was awful. We hardly talked except for me yelling things like, 'Keep a tight rein!' I decided to forget it all.

"Now, you might think I decided at that point to drop him, right? Wrong. Now (six months later), I'm 16, and he's pushing 21. I like him again—I think! The big thing is that he is quiet but realistic. He loves God a lot—though he doesn't go around preaching. He seriously acknowledges his Christianity. And that's so important to me. Oh, and he doesn't even dress HOT like he used to. I think God has been showing me that you can't idolize guys. You have to see them as people. Then you can let feelings come in. Even if we never have anything, at least the wall was broken and I'll have a friend who will always be there. And true friends are all that count."

COMMITMENT

The second principle is commitment. You might think this is an odd suggestion too, because the very nature of dating is, in a sense, uncommitted. Dating is a trial period. You're trying to find out how well you like each other.

But beneath the "trial" should be a firm commitment to the love and caring of a friendship. Commitment means caring for your partner enough to ensure that there is nothing to regret later. Once you begin caring for someone you don't just stop because it becomes difficult, or because the relationship changes. You're committed—not to the relationship, but to the person's welfare.

This doesn't mean you should stick with the same person forever. What it does mean is that after a breakup you should continue talking to each other, caring about each other. If you can't do that, what kind of relationship did you have in the first place?

We'll talk more about breaking up in a later chapter, but I need to add one thing now to balance what I've just said: It may be impossible to relate to each other immediately after a breakup, because emotions do need time to cool. But there are plenty of chances later.

COMMUNICATION

When a *Campus Life* survey asked readers to identify what their biggest dating concerns were, both guys and girls listed "knowing how to communicate" at the top (49 percent for girls, 71 percent for the guys—guys know they need help in this area!). Communication is the third principle of a good relationship. The following letter illustrates the problem.

I started going out with a girl about five months ago. Our relationship looked great in the beginning, but soon school vacation came and we didn't see much of each other except at church events.

Now we're on the phone a lot, but we never really talk about anything important. And we don't talk much when we're together. I've heard that communication is essential for making a relationship work. I can't see much communication in ours. Don't tell me to just go over and talk to her because it's harder than that. But I really want to make this relationship work.

This relationship sounds very typical: two people are attracted to each other, and for a while everything looked great. The Plus side of dating brought them together.

Now, however, this guy is realizing that it takes more to make a relationship. He senses that if two unique people are to relate together in genuine love, they must try to understand each other—understand how they're different as well as how they're alike. That takes communication. Great

"But enough about me. Let's talk about cars!"

feelings, comfortable silences, having fun together—these are no substitute for communication.

But few people are naturally good communicators. Communication is not the same as talking a lot. It has more to do with listening carefully. You must explore new ground—not just make noises about the things you've been doing. Communication requires that you put into words the ideas and feelings you've always taken for granted—those ideas you thought everybody shared, but which your partner does not. Communication is, therefore, hard work for most people.

First I'll tell you what not to do. When two people are mutually attracted but can't find anything to say, they're tempted to fill in the silence by getting physical. I remember one boyfriend named Chuck with whom that happened. He was not very talkative, but he was affectionate! At first hugging and kissing made me feel closer to him. But very soon I began to feel used. Why wouldn't he talk to me? Why did he just want to make out? Soon enough, the relationship was over.

I learned that making out never substitutes for communication. I've seen other cases where people tried to make it a substitute and they "stayed together," but their love was hollow.

How to talk? There are no magic secrets, only practice, practice, practice. Like learning basketball, you feel awkward at first. You just have to keep practicing until it begins to feel smooth.

Here are a few hints that might help:

1. Keep your practice sessions short and frequent. It's much easier to talk every day for five minutes than once a week for two hours.

2. Carry a notebook and jot down thoughts you'd like to communicate so your partner can understand you better. Keep track of feelings, opinions, conversations that come up

in the events of the day. Then, when you talk, just go through the list. You might suggest your friend do the same.

3. Learn to ask questions that will get your friend to share feelings and opinions. You can jot these down in your notebook too. "What did you do today?" is a poor question. "What did you do in basketball today?" is a mediocre question. "How does the basketball coach act in practice?" is a better question. "What is it about basketball that you like?" is another.

4. Share spiritually, by telling each other what you learned from the Bible (no matter how small), and by praying for each other in specific ways about activities and problems you have talked about. Then you're not just communicating to understand each other. You're communicating in order to help, and that fosters closeness.

OK, now we've got the ingredients of a good relationship—Friendship Plus God, based on acceptance, commitment, and communication. The question remains: What should you actually do on a date to foster all these wonderful things and bring you closer to understanding what the Dream is all about? That's what we'll consider next.

11. *Creative Dates*

I wish we could go back to doing something really silly, like
fingerpaint, like we used to do when we were eight or nine.
                  —*Don, high school student, Massachusetts*

All the things we like to do are things we did when we were
little kids. We try to capture a little bit of the time when we
didn't have any obligations or responsibilities. Spending a
little time like that rejuvenates you.
                       —*Amy, college student, Illinois*

What makes for a great date? As Julie, a college student
from Illinois, says, "An ideal date doesn't mean spending a
lot of money." What makes memorable times? Being
together, having fun and, often, learning something together.

I asked *Campus Life* readers to send in their best ideas for
creative dates, in several categories. I took the most unusual
ideas I found, and left out the more typical ideas (for
example, watching or participating in sports, going for a
walk, going to the movies, driving around, going to a dance
or to a party, renting a video, playing games at home, etc.).
There's nothing wrong with any of these ideas, but most
people think of them. I wanted to offer ideas that were
either very unusual in themselves, or offered a different
twist to a more common activity.

Take what you think looks good, try it, modify it—and
have fun! Remember, it's OK to want to go out in order to
have fun. God created us with the ability to laugh.

DATES FOR PAUPERS (NO CASH NEEDED) ─────

My boyfriend and I enjoy looking at model or new or still-being-built homes. It's fun to admire the beautiful ones and think about which one best fits each of our ideas of a dream house. This can be done just as a couple or with other couples and friends.

Because my boyfriend and I live far apart, our times together usually consist of visits which occur while one of us must be in school (college). When I'm at his school, I go to classes with him, instead of hanging around elsewhere. He goes to my classes, too, when he visits me. You can't beat the cost, and it gives us a taste of what the other is doing in school. Also, it's a change of pace from our regular school grind, and a chance to learn something new!

—*Sandra Partlow, Annandale, New Jersey*

Leave an entire day free, and start the date in the morning by getting together in the kitchen. Using only what is available, make The Best Picnic Lunch Ever, including dessert. Then, by way of foot or bicycle, go to an area of a highway where there is a wide, grassy median. Go to the median, spread out a blanket, and enjoy your feast. It's great for publicity!

—*Tina Holden, Gurnee, Illinois*

Call a friend who's moved away and surprise them.

Watch slides or look at pictures of each other's families while you eat popcorn.

—*Kate Rockey, Kennewick, Washington)*

Wash a car together. I know my date and I have had a lot of fun squirting each other!

—*Jayne Bammel, Kerrville, Texas*

My boyfriend started reading me "bedtime" stories every night. (Most people have old children's books around the house so you don't have to buy new books. Or you could check some old favorites out of a library.) We learned what each other's favorite children's books were, and we also learned about each other's childhood.

Another idea: we decorated blown-out eggs. We put a pin hole in both ends of the egg and blew the insides out. Then we took magic markers and drew on the eggs. It was fun to be creative, and we enjoyed doing it together, too!

My boyfriend and I visited a cemetery. The sayings on the gravestones were interesting to read, and we learned what time periods interested the other person.

—*Melissa Moses, Rochester, New Hampshire*

If both you and your date enjoy kids, take a Saturday afternoon and visit a children's hospital or home near you. Spend the day playing games with the kids and getting to know them. They love the attention, and it's a neat way to find out more about young children. Afterward, you and your date can go somewhere and spend some time alone discussing how your day went. (This could also be a group date.)

—*Jody Eckert, Phillips, Wisconsin*

Put on some dirty, shabby clothes and go down to the city together and notice how people stare at you. It will be fun to cause a stir; maybe you could even try to get in to a fancy restaurant. You'll have a different kind of fun and learn about others, yourself, and your date!

—*Laura Marth*

If both members of the dating couple are interested in not only saving, but making money, they could consider this plan. The local Plasma Alliance will offer anywhere from ten to twenty-five dollars for plasma donations. This procedure takes a few hours, during which time the donor shares a couch with another (in this case, their date). This is an interesting situation to be in. It allows the people on the date to talk while performing a much-needed community service. After the donation is made, the couple can go out to dinner, using the money they made from the donation. This is a great way to get to know someone right to the core.

—*Susan Wilbers, Mexico, Missouri*

Do a jigsaw puzzle—the larger the better (requires more dates to complete the puzzle!). Listening to music, sharing some silences, talking, and puzzle solving can be a great way to "get to know you."

Plan a garage sale for your families. (Helps clean out garages and attics, plus you can earn some money, too!) Window-shop at the dog pound or pet store.
—*Cyndy Sadleir, Westhampton, New York*

Check out a bird book from the library, borrow a pair or two of binoculars, and go bird watching. Best times: mid-April through mid-May, and in the fall.

If you prefer plants or trees, see how many you can identify correctly. Bring a field guide to learn new species.

Spread a blanket on top of a hill with a pretty view. Give yourselves an hour to write a poem for each other. You don't necessarily have to make the words rhyme. If you think you can't write a poem, do it anyway. You'll surprise yourself.

CHEAP DATES

Go sightseeing in your own city. Chances are you generally don't see the interesting tourist attractions because they're no big deal to you. You'll probably find them much more interesting than when you were four!
—*Ellen Riggsbee, Waukesha, Wisconsin*

I only recommend this if you know each other very well. Go to one or the other person's house and get out the old baby pictures. It's great to reminisce; besides, any mom will be just thrilled to get them out, along with any embarrassing anecdotes!
—*Francie Huffstetler, Williamsburg, Virginia*

Turn a shopping trip to the mall into an inexpensive date. Give your date an imaginary $100 (any amount will do) and see what he or she would buy. Or agree to spend no more than a certain amount of money and go off and try to find a surprise gift for your date. If whatever you each select doesn't fit or match any color known to man, it can be returned on the spot.

Go to the zoo. Spend an afternoon roaming around looking at all the animals. Rename the animals after people you know.
—*Sharla Berget, Bismarck, North Dakota*

Mike quickly decided that this would be his last date with Zelda Laslow, president of the sky diving club.

Materials needed: wood, appropriate tools, picnic basket, food, blanket (optional: candles, matches, radio).

This date is an all-day Saturday excursion. First, one of the parties involved must volunteer a tree from his or her back yard. (The tree should be rather large.) The other party will collect needed materials and set the day for the date.

Early Saturday morning, the person with the materials arrives at the person with the tree's backyard. The two then start their project: building a simple, platform treehouse in the tree. Throughout the day, the two dates work side by side to complete the work of love. They will probably get to know one another very well during the course of the day! After the treehouse is completed, the two share a picnic dinner on the platform. The dinner can be enhanced by music from a portable radio and candles.

—Dena Ratliff, Dumas, Texas

One date I had which only required gas and Coke money was a Sunday or Saturday afternoon at the nearest large airport. We drove to the airport and walked to the window with the best view of the planes taking off and landing. We drank a Coke and visited for two hours. We "people watched" and talked about how different God made everyone. The day was most enjoyable and very, very inexpensive.

—Brooke Breed, San Marcos, Texas

An inexpensive way to really get to know someone is to make a "baking date": Invite the girl or guy of your attentions to your place to bake cookies or paraffin balls or something else that takes awhile to make. Then after your baking is done, break out a game of "Risk" or "Life" (no need to be real competitive) and enjoy your new creation. This is a good way to show you're not some "macho he-man," and it gives you an excellent opportunity to talk and get to know each other.

—Rodney Weed, Palmer, Alaska

Buy $5 worth of public transportation tickets and see how far you can go (and still get back).

CHILDHOOD REVISITED

A fun date which does not have to cost any money at all is a trip to a large toy store. It's fun to relive childhood memories. It is interesting to discover what toys you both played with. My boyfriend and I discovered that we both played with Lincoln Logs most of the time! It is also fun to see what new toys have come about since we were kids. In lots of toy stores, people can play with the electronic equipment, and that is a lot of fun, too. At the end of the date to the toy store, it is fun to buy each other little gifts such as bubbles or "Scientific Glowing Glop"!

Another fun date, which is another place mainly meant for children, is one of those "please touch" museums. Most cities have one. We went to the Franklin Institute in Philadelphia, and for a whole day it only cost us $4 each. It was fun walking through the giant human heart, playing with pendulums and weights and even with electricity!

—*Molly S. Probst, Dillsburg, Pennsylvania*

This date begins in the toy department at the local Wal-Mart. All you need is a bottle of soap bubbles, blower included in the bottle. This usually costs less than $1. If you are tempted to invest in those newfangled bubble kits with the multibubble blowers, don't waste the money; they're not any more fun than the old-fashioned blower-in-the-bottle.

Location is very important in a bubble-blowing excursion. During the day, an ideal spot would be in a park or beside a lake. (If there are ducks in the lake, it's fun to tease them with the bubbles!) At night, a most romantic spot to bubble blow is near a public fountain with colored lights. These lights transform the bubbles into diamonds, dreams, or a multitude of objects—your imagination is the only limit.

Warnings: Bubble blowing is addictive. Bubbles may not form well in very cold weather or in the wind. Don't try to color the soap with food coloring; it is too heavy and forms a blob of color at the bottom of the bubble which tends to fall on indignant ducks—not pretty. Whatever you do, be creative! This "dying art" should be turned into an international sport.

—*Jennifer Orr, Pineville, Louisiana*

Go to a park and bring a set of kiddy watercolors and brushes and lots of paper and paint your hearts out (flowers, trees, clouds, etc.). Compare pictures with your date. Even if you're not an artist, you can enjoy a good laugh.

—*Trisha Bowker, Hillsboro, Oregon*

Round up each other's best baby photos and visit a do-it-yourself frame shop. Frame your own, then exchange them for gifts.

VARIATIONS ON AN OLD FAVORITE: THE PICNIC

For a very special, romantic date, try packing a picnic basket and going on a picnic. On this picnic, however, don't bring hot dogs, chips, and Coke. Pack fried chicken (it can be cold or kept warm by putting it into a dish and wrapping the dish with towels to insulate it). Also, bring fresh strawberries, grapes, Welch's sparkling grape juice, cheese, and for dessert, chocolate eclairs. Leave the plasticware at home and use your best silverware and prettiest dishes. For the Welch's bubbly bring champagne or wine glasses. Before you eat, go out and pick wildflowers and put them in a vase for a centerpiece. Don't forget a blanket to sit on. The best place for your romantic picnic is a secluded, grassy field, not a public park. The most romantic time of day to go is right before sunset. Surprise your guy/gal by keeping the date a secret. Blindfold him or her for the last part of the drive out there. I did this for my boyfriend's birthday one evening last spring and he loved it.

—*Jill Christopherson, Coppell, Texas*

Take a camera and try some "nature photography"—flowers, trees, whatever! Pretend you're out on assignment for *National Geographic* and try to be really creative! You'd be surprised at how good pictures can turn out with practice. Take pictures of one another, too—and then enjoy your picnic lunch.

—*Kim Knack, Phoenix, Arizona*

If you plan a picnic and it rains, don't let the weather ruin your plans! A little creativity will save the date. Make a huge yellow "sun" out of posterboard and hang it in the garage. Set up lounge chairs and the big blanket and let the scene begin. Oh, yeah! Don't forget your sunglasses!

—*Francie Huffstetler, Williamsburg, Virginia*

Other activities you can plan along with a picnic: horseback riding; bike riding; hiking; boating; sailing; swimming; frisbee, charades; read aloud to each other.

GROUP DATES

Who says a date has to be just with one other person? In fact, some people prefer group dating, especially when you are just getting to know someone. Having others to talk to can increase the fun and cut down on the tension. Girls

CHUCK AND PETE DID NOT CARE FOR GLENDA'S
VERSION OF DOUBLE-DATING.

usually feel less inhibited about inviting some guy they like to a group activity. And anyone can initiate a group date.

For this date you need seven couples. Each couple needs to pitch in and help rent one video camera (unless you can borrow one elsewhere). At the agreed upon time and place, have each couple draw one slip of paper out of a hat. On the slips of paper there will be one of the following titles: sportscasters, weathercasters, video camera couple, TV chefs, newscasters, bathroom bowl cleaner commercial, and denture cleaner commercial. You can substitute other ideas if you prefer. Each couple has ten or fifteen minutes to prepare their performance imitating the people on their slips of paper. (This is a good time for the video camera couple to get some behind-the-scenes candid shots.) When the ten minutes are up, the couples are taped in the following sequence by the video camera couple: newscasters, sportscasters, weather forecasters, one of the commercials, then the two TV chefs, the other commercial, and the last news recap. After all the scripts and taping are done, everyone helps make some popcorn and drinks and then sits down to watch themselves on TV.

—*Dee Muraski, Warsaw, Indiana*

Have a mud fight with a bunch of people.

—*Trisha Bowker, Hillsboro, Oregon*

Two guys I knew made up slips of paper with quotes on them (poems they made up) giving their dates clues where to go. They picked up the girls, gave them the papers, and waited while they guessed where they were supposed to go next. They went all over the city of Birmingham. When they got to the last clue they were given clues and a map, and they had to find three points on the map where they were to go next. That took them out to our house where there was a lake and woods. They went in a boat around to a point in the lake, got out, built a fire, roasted marshmallows, and sang till early morning. The girls said they both loved it.

—*Lisa Lewis, Chelsea, Alabama*

I'm part of a girl's Bible study at my university, and once we got together and planned a great group date. Each girl picked a Christian guy from our fellowship. We had the Bible study leader inform each guy that they were being "kidnapped" by a group of girls Friday night. They were told to meet at a particular site on campus and wait for further instructions. Each girl dressed in a borrowed trench coat and cap, wore dark sunglasses, and came armed with squirt guns and bandannas. We ambushed the guys, blindfolded them, and marched them to the "get-away" cars. They had no idea where they were going. We drove them to this huge hill lit by spotlights, which offers an incredible view of our city. Some of us had gone ahead and set up blankets and baskets of cheese, grapes, and warm French bread. There was also soft classical music playing and chilled, sparkling cider. After talking for a while, and a quick game of football (girls vs. guys, of course), we had a Domino's pizza delivered to our hill. A fun time was had by all!

—*Martha Thresher, Towson, Maryland*

Hector's attempt to impress Martha Crinstein with fancy French cuisine appeared doomed to failure.

Get together one or two couples besides you and your date and have fun at home! Get all the girls (or guys) together to fix a fancy dinner. Each person can bring a part of the meal (for example, someone can bring a salad and another can bring dessert). You can make the main dish together. A nice touch is preparing a beautifully set table with all the trimmings of a restaurant table (good dishes, along with special napkins, water glasses, etc.). Whoever prepared the meal can serve the others as if they were at a restaurant.

—*Julie Rowe, Columbus, Ohio*

Take a walking tour of your hometown and be sure to bring your cameras! (Polaroids are most fun, but any camera will do.) See who can find the most creative subjects to photograph, e.g., one or more couples in the local phone booth, playing on the playground, or attempting to order at the drive-through of your local McDonald's. Use your imagination! One plus of not using Polaroids is that when the pictures come back, you can have another group date. Invite the gang over, pop some popcorn, and make looking at your artistic endeavors a mini-party.

—*Bobbi Dykema, Strasburg, North Dakota*

PROM AND OTHER SPECIAL OCCASIONS ────────

Tired of spending $50 on the traditional prom dinner at "The Hotel"? Try a McProm! You and your date, looking spiffy in your tux and gown, enter McDonald's carrying a picnic basket containing the following: two champagne glasses, two plates (preferably china), two sets of silverware, two place mats, two long candles and candlesticks, matches, a small tape recorder, and a tape of your favorite classical music. Walk elegantly to the counter and order your favorite Mickey Dee's food in a French accent. Retreat to the most secluded of the booths (preferably by a window), arrange your table setting, light the candles, transfer your burgers from the brightly colored wrapping to the plates, pour the Cokes into the champagne glass, hit the play button, and sit back and enjoy the true McProm experience.

—*Wendy Birch, Amherst, Massachusetts*

Note: The above idea can also be adapted for a group date, according to Tina Holden of Gurnee, Illinois and Sandra Partlow of Annandale, New Jersey. You would get a group together, all dress up formal (gives the girls a chance to wear their prom dresses again), set up the tables, play the music, etc. Tina advises to make sure you climax the evening by playing on the McDonald-land playground.

What to do that's fun after the prom? Kerri Bobo of Springfield, Ohio and Matthew Stoddard of Fairgrove, Michigan advocate miniature golf. "It may have looked odd to those around, with us in our high heels, tie and all," says Kerri, "but we had a great time and were the best dressed there!" Matthew advises going out for banana splits or sundaes after shooting the course. "It was a prom I'll never forget!" he says.

Last year my boyfriend and I decided we wanted to do something creative for the prom. So he said he would surprise me, and he did just that. When he picked me up for "the big evening," he said nothing about what we were going to do. I was dying of curiosity! He kept driving until we hit the country. We then turned onto a dirt road that led to a small lake. We parked the car by the dock on the lake.

He led me over to one of the rowboats along the dock and we got in. (It was tricky with my prom dress!) We started rowing across the lake. Then, in the middle of the lake, he picked up his guitar that was lying in the rowboat and started singing and playing for me. He then rowed until we came to the other side of the lake. We got out and were greeted by my boyfriend's older brother and his girlfriend, dressed in black bow ties and white shirts and black pants. They led us onto a wooden footbridge that stretched across the lake. There on the bridge was a table set with fine china. The "waiters" asked us to be seated. They proceeded to serve us a wonderful meal. After the meal, we rowed back over the lake and drove to where the prom was being held. It was a wonderful evening.

—*Trisha Bowker, Hillsboro, Oregon*

THIS WAS NOT THE ROMANTIC DINNER
THAT LOUISE HAD ENVISIONED FOR PROM NIGHT.

12. *What Is True Love?*

I have known this guy for about five years. About two months ago we really noticed each other. We've been going together for these past two months. I really think I love this guy (I'm only 14). And he loves me.

We're both Christians and have God as the center of our lives. We pray for each other and our relationship. And we've confessed to each other that if it's God's will, we will marry. My parents pray for me and my relationship with him.

Is it too early to tell if it's true love? If it is true love, how can we be certain? I don't want to say or do something that we'll both regret for a long time.

How do you know you're really in love? How do you know when you've found the right person, a person who can make the Dream a reality with you?

A 19-year-old guy named Joe told me, "Most everyone defines love differently. Some say love is a decision, some say it is a feeling, others say it's a tingling sensation, and still others say it 'just happens.' I believe love isn't an 'instant happening' like live news coverage; love is something that grows. I believe that you know you are really in love when you are willing to put the other person ahead of yourself. I know that I am in love with a girl when she becomes more important than my own existence."

"I think if you are really in love," said Andy, a high-school senior from Colorado, "you will have a genuine concern for your partner's needs above and before your own. You want the best for them, regardless of what that means to you."

"I think love starts out with just two people mutually taking an interest in each other," said a girl from Illinois. "You start doing things that you wouldn't normally do, and you have a sudden concern about what the other person thinks so you want to make good impressions." After thinking a moment, she added, "I think you're really in love, though, when you no longer have to try to impress but can be content with and depend on each other."

"True love is when you love that person for who they are, not based on looks, or status, or anything else," said Tanya.

"I think it's when you're willing to be committed to that person and loving them when they are at their worst as well as their best," said Diane, a senior from Minnesota.

Most people recognize that true love is something that grows. "Instant 'love' cannot hold, because more than likely it's just infatuation," Amy told me. A guy from North Carolina said, "There is a feeling of closeness that comes over you and grows stronger with time." And Laurie speculated, "I think (though I can't know since I don't feel I've ever been in love) that love sort of creeps up on you."

There's comfort and security when you're really in love. Allison told me, "I can honestly say that I am really in love with my best friend. There is just a sense of security and comfort whenever I see him, talk to him, or even talk about him. He's always there for me. I can talk to him about anything that is on my mind. I'm never nervous around him and he is not nervous around me, either."

Allison makes a good point. There is a popular conception of love, portrayed again and again in songs and soap operas, that love is linked with suffering. "I can't live, with or without you," U2 sang. Lots of highly-charged experiences and emotions have been linked with love, but they may not have anything to do with love at all.

IN LOVE WITH RICK

I remember the first time I was in love. It started as Friendship, with no initial "Plus" attraction. Somehow, slowly, the relationship became a Friendship Plus kind of thing.

There was that strange stage when I wasn't sure what Rick was feeling—or even what I was feeling. I remember the secret pain of seeing him go out with other people. The awkwardness of finally bringing up my feelings. The agony of waiting for Rick to respond. The joy when we did finally go out. The fun and happy and special times. We shared a love for God, a faith that gave our lives meaning and direction.

He was not especially good-looking, but I loved his looks because they were so Rick. I cared about what he felt, did, thought. It was intense; I felt I loved him more than I loved myself. I wanted only the best for him. I hurt when he hurt. A special hope sprang to life as we began to talk about a future together, as we began to dream the Dream together.

But then the confusion and hurt came, when he pulled back again and again. We broke up, we came back. We tried to keep at least a friendship alive, through all the wrenching turmoil of our relationship.

And suddenly, it was over. Finally and for good.

That was one of the most painful relationships I ever experienced. It taught me a lot.

For one thing, it taught me that we make choices in love relationships. Choices that can lead either to shortcuts to the Dream or to side roads away from that final hoped-for destination. Being in love is not enough. We have to cultivate that love.

Part of our problem in figuring out love, I think, is that we have only one word for a wide range of feelings and experiences. The Greeks were smarter. They had four words. C. S. Lewis elaborates on each of these in his book *The Four Loves.*

One kind of love, what we usually mean when we say we "fell in love," is *eros.* Lewis defines eros as "a delighted preoccupation with the Beloved." It's that sense that you don't want to live without the other person. You would do

"I'M STARTING TO HAVE LITTLE NAGGING DOUBTS ABOUT ROGER. HIS LETTER BEGINS, 'MY ONE AND ONLY DARLING PAMELA — OR CURRENT RESIDENT'..."

anything for the person. You crave to be with him or her. There's an intensity of emotion, and a spark of attraction— though sexual attraction is only one part of eros. In ancient literature Cupid was the messenger of eros, flinging his arrows where he would. Eros seems to have its own logic, setting reason aside. By its very nature, eros is both intense and fickle. It seems to sweep us away in a wave of feeling—

but, like ocean waves, eros follows its own rhythm of ebb and flow.

Eros needs other kinds of love to sustain it, if it's to last more than a week and grow into something solid. One love that could fit this is *storge,* which translated from the Greek is affection. It's the kind of love your parents feel for you, and you feel for your parents. It's also the kind of love you can feel for an old friend, a sibling, your next-door neighbor that you've known forever, or even a pet. There's a warm comfortableness, a homey satisfaction in being together. Affection is bred in familiarity. You know affection is part of your relationship when you're unafraid to wear your oldest jeans around her; when you feel OK about letting him see you without makeup once in a while. If your parents have been married for quite a while, chances are their love has a large element of affection in it. This love makes the other loves "wear well."

FRIENDSHIP LOVE

A third kind of love is called *philia*. It's at the basis of most budding friendships. These relationships happen when two people find they have some special third thing in common. Philia is that excitement that comes when you find out that someone sees the same truth you do, or cares about the same thing. ("I don't believe it, you like jazz too! I thought I was the only one.") Friendship, in this sense, must be *about* something, even if it's getting through trigonometry together.

Philia is distinct from eros in a couple of ways. Friends hardly ever talk about the friendship itself; they're too preoccupied with their common interests. But lovers are always talking to one another about their love. Lovers are normally face to face, absorbed in each other; friends are side by side, absorbed in some common interest. That's why it's so awkward if you like someone as a friend, and your friend starts to feel something more (eros); you're not looking at your friend, not preoccupied with the relationship, but your friend is beginning to look at you in that special way.

Another thing about friendship versus eros: Eros is restricted to two people; but friendship-love gets more out of being shared with others. Isn't it true that different friends bring different parts of you to light? With one friend, your clownish self might come out; with another, your more serious, sensitive side. If you're truly a Friend with someone, you enjoy seeing all these sides of him or her. The addition of other people to the relationship enriches, rather than threatens, it.

" Bob, I've been thinking... perhaps our relationship has become too casual."

The fourth and last love is *agape*, a very special kind of love. It's what I call choice-love. It's the love that is there in moments when eros cools; when you and your friend aren't gazing at your common passion; when even affection isn't strong enough. The other loves more or less happen. Eros is something you "fall into," friendship is sparked by common interests, and affection grows from familiarity. All of these "natural loves" can be bound together and transformed by choice-love. Agape doesn't just "happen"; you make it happen.

First Corinthians 13, that famous "love chapter," describes choice-love: "Love is patient, love is kind. It does not envy, it does not boast, it is not proud. It is not rude, it is not self-seeking, it is not easily angered, it keeps no record of wrongs. Love does not delight in evil but rejoices with the truth. It always protects, always trusts, always hopes, always perseveres. Love never fails."

I call it choice-love because it is based on actions, not feelings. You choose to be patient when your girlfriend is late and you may miss the movie. When your boyfriend gets a better grade on his test than you, you choose to rejoice with him. You choose not to seek your own pleasure when your hormones are screaming for you to keep going. You choose to forgive when your lover hurts your feelings—or even breaks up with you.

Choice-love means that, all through the relationship, you choose the best for the person, the relationship, and yourself. It means you keep the Dream before you, and do nothing that will keep you or your partner from someday reaching that destination, whether together, or with other partners.

Another term for choice-love might be commitment-love. You commit yourself to seeking the best for the person, the relationship, and yourself.

THE LOVES BRAIDED TOGETHER

I have a braided belt which reminds me of love in all its facets. This belt is made out of yarns of different colors. The green strands are coarse and strong. Other strands are more delicate, like the bright, light-blue strands, tied with little knots. Another strand is fuchsia; it too is thin and delicate, unknotted. There are twisted white strands, and twisted and knotted light-blue strands. All are braided together to make a belt that has light and dark, bright and muted colors in it.

I think of love in this way. Each aspect of life that is shared with another person on a deep level of mutual trust and commitment is like a strand that makes up the whole relationship. The more you share—the more bonds you have—the stronger, more colorful, and textured your relationship is.

Some strands are stronger than others. The bonds formed by mutual commitment and a shared faith give strength and stability to the relationship. Shared values add both strength and texture, like the twisted and knotted strands of my belt. Common interests, common friends, trust, communication—all of these add their colors and textures. Each relationship has its own braided pattern. That is the beauty, and mystery, of love.

Sex, and the attraction I have labeled "Plus," is like that one lone fuchsia thread in my belt. By itself it is just a delicate strand, unable to hold anything together. But woven with the other strands, it adds beauty and variety to the belt.

Unfortunately, many of us let the whole relationship hang on that one fragile strand. The wonderful, wild feelings of eros sweep us away. We forget we have a choice.

I remember when my best friend was in love with a guy. Because she was in love with him she thought she should marry him. Carla asked me one day whether I agreed. Being her best friend, I thought I should be honest. I said, slowly, "No, because he doesn't have the same goals as you do. You said you wanted to go to college. He doesn't. You seem to be more intellectual than him, you like to think about things, and he doesn't seem interested in that."

Carla seemed offended. "But we're in love," she pointed out. I didn't say anything more. At the time, there was nothing to say. Eros had its own logic. Who knows, the reasoning went, you might not fall in love again, and then you would have blown your chances. I didn't realize that it's fairly commonplace to fall in love, and that intelligent choices needed to be made in response to feelings.

Carla did learn this, I think, but the hard way, when her marriage fell apart.

13. *Cathy and Rodney: Choice-Love in Action*

> I had never had a guy respect me so much. I was just amazed at that. Rodney was so sensitive and patient. It was definitely a different experience for me. It made me realize that you can't settle for second-best in a relationship.
>
> —*Cathy*

When I began writing this book, I asked many people to recommend couples whose relationship seemed especially healthy and alive. I wanted to talk to them and get a picture of what a great relationship looks like, how it started, how it developed, the choices that led toward their dream. I spoke to a number of couples, but none impressed me as much as Cathy Smith and Rodney Duttweiler.

Cathy and Rodney had just finished their senior year at a midwestern Christian college when I met them. They were engaged, and about to be married in just a few weeks. Cathy was pretty, with smooth dark hair, big blue eyes, and an impish smile. Rodney looked like a football player, big, broad-shouldered, but with a boyish face. Rodney struck me as the cautious, thoughtful type, and he was soft-spoken. Cathy's style was energetic and open. They were obviously in love, but I wanted to test the depth and texture of that love. What kind of a foundation were they building their dream on? I started by asking them how their relationship began.

Rodney: I met Cathy in my New Testament class. One of my roommates told me he had met this great girl and that he was going to date her. I asked him who she was and he said, "Cathy Smith." Sometime in the next few days I ended up sitting next to her in class. The class was talking about missions and being really committed to following Christ. After class, I asked Cathy if she would like to get together and talk sometime.

We got together the next Wednesday and started talking, and for the next month, every Wednesday we would get together and just talk.

Cathy: We started out being just friends. I wasn't especially "attracted" to him and I don't think he was "attracted" to me in a flirtatious kind of way.

Rodney: But I really enjoyed talking to her.

Cathy: We would talk about our families. My family is very important to me, and he had that same value in family and relationships. It was special to talk to someone who understood where I was coming from. We just really hit it off as friends. We must have talked about three hours that first time we got together.

We never used the word "date" at all. Dates, to our thinking, were superficial, so we said, "Let's get together and talk."

Rodney: Here at this college, it seems that if a guy and girl are together it's automatically dating. And if you're together you're going to be married. I believe people probably said that about Cathy and me, but we talked about it and decided to ignore it. All this kind of pressure really is a bad thing. So many people are controlled by it.

Cathy: We talked about what we expected from a relationship maybe the second time we talked. We were both more interested at that stage in putting Christ first in our lives; that was our main goal. God must have been in the relationship all the way, because I look back and I can't believe that we went so slowly! It would have been easy for me to jump in and cling to somebody—I'd done that before. But Rodney was really on target and really stable. I looked up to him and respected him and he respected me, which is an incredible thing, because guys just don't respect girls.

Rodney: After we finally began going together we had to consciously make a decision to keep our eyes on God. We had to keep reminding ourselves, discussing it, and praying about it. There were times when we weren't doing too well on the spiritual side of things.

Cathy: And you could tell because our relationship would be all jumpy and we would get angry with each other for dumb things. Then we would immediately say, "How are we doing with God?" We were constantly making sure and checking up with each other, not in a critical way but in a loving way.

Rodney: When we prayed together that really helped. It would help to hear each other voice to God our desire to keep him in the center.

Cathy: I would write him poetry. I would also call him up first thing in the morning just to say hi. I think that surprising the other person is nice. It really shows that you don't think of them only when they are with you. You care enough to do something out of the ordinary. He would give me a rose in the middle of the week, even though he didn't have much money. He tried to show how much he cared for me as a friend in as many different ways that he could.

Tell me about how your relationship turned from friendship to something more than friends. Did it happen at the same time for each of you?

Cathy: We had reached a point where we had to talk about where our relationship was headed. Were we just friends, or what were we?

I thought for sure he was going to say, "Cathy, I just don't think you're the one for me; we just better cool it." I knew it was coming, but he told me that he was interested in me and really cared for me.

It was a while before he said he actually loved me. We didn't want to jump ahead and say things before we knew what they meant. Saying we'd be more than friends was just one step. We were slowly moving forward.

A lot of times we'd get together just to talk. Anytime something came up that we were uncomfortable about we would talk about it. There were no guessing games. I hate it when you have to guess what the other person is thinking and then you just end up going in two different directions.

My parents [who are missionaries] were on furlough that year and I lived at home, just down from the college. He lived at one of the dorms. It was really neat to have my parents around because they only come back every three years. They were able to see me in that process of getting to know Rodney. They knew right away that something was different about him because I acted differently. My mother used to worry about some of the guys I dated.

116

How did some of your past dating experiences affect your relationship?

Cathy: I never really had a boyfriend until I came back to the States one year and started dating a guy who was a year older than I was. He was a junior in high school so he was already looking for something a little more serious. I was not at all. We never communicated about that. I would just have fun flirting with other guys.

Then I went back to Africa to finish my high school. I came to college my freshman year and suffered culture shock. I went through a lot of hard times. I got in with the wrong crowd and was dating a guy who was not even a Christian. He really dragged me down.

A lot of my relationships were very physical. I desired so much for someone to love me for who I was that I would just take anybody. I guess I didn't have much respect for myself. I was depressed a lot of the time. Some of that was because I was separated from my parents; it was my first year in college; I had no one to talk to, so it was easy to get involved in those kinds of relationships.

At the end of the school year I realized that this was not the way I want to live. I decided I wasn't going to date any more guys. But that summer I got involved in a relationship and again, as in my other relationships, I was the stabilizing force. The guys just clung to me, which is unusual. Usually it's the girls clinging to the guys.

After that I said, "God, I'm just sick of this. I'm tired of relationships. I put it in your hands. I want to be dedicated to you and you alone." At the beginning of the next school year I had guys ask me out on dates and I felt the freedom to tell them I was interested in being friends but that I wasn't interested in anything else.

Then I met Rodney. I had never had a guy respect me so much. I was just amazed at that. He was so sensitive and so patient. It was definitely a different situation than before. It made me realize that you can't settle for second-best. It's not worth the hurt, the pain, and the memories of why you did certain things.

Rodney: I didn't date that much until high school, and then I dated one girl for three years. I thought it was a really good relationship in a lot of ways, but I also got hurt a lot. I found out much later that she had cheated on me. When I came to college I was still dating her, but after only about two months I realized that the relationship was holding me down in my Christian growth.

In high school I was captain of the football team and she was captain of the cheerleaders. We were on the phone with each other all the time. It was a real fairy-tale kind of thing. I remember even asking my mom, "Mom, what would happen if we got married?" In my hometown that would be the thing to do. It's a real country town where people go to church, meet someone, get married, have families, and stay there the rest of their lives.

Actually, she was the one who called me and broke up. I didn't want to be the one to break it. I was afraid of hurting her.

Then I stayed away from dating. I committed in my heart, "God, I'm not going to date anyone until I know you better." So I didn't date. I had a lot of friends—girl friends.

Then Cathy came along. At first I just wanted to talk, but after a couple of times of talking I was convinced that this was going to be something. I was intrigued by her. I grew up in one place my whole life, but Cathy had lived in Vietnam and Africa and all over the world—that intrigued me. And the way she loved people and her desire to serve God; I hadn't seen that in other girls. It was really exciting.

Cathy: He knew he was called to the mission field, and I knew I was called to missions, so I knew I could not end up marrying somebody that had not had the same calling.

Rodney: I had gone with some girls who had said that they would go to the mission field if their husband was called. I talked to my dad about that. He said, "Marry someone who is called to be a missionary. Don't waste your time dating someone who you know wouldn't have that call."

Cathy: At first it was the spiritual attraction alone that drew me to Rodney. I was not attracted to him physically at all. But the fact that he was so Christ-like just blew me away. And the fact that he wanted to talk to me blew me away. I mean, why me?

It's funny because I always used to say that I was going to end up marrying someone who grew up overseas. I would never marry an American. And he was an American to the core. He had never been anywhere at all except in the United States. And he was a football player, and I did not like football players. I thought those guys were just so stuck up and all they thought about were their bodies. He changed all my ideas about an American football player who lived in a small town all his life.

Rod is a very giving person. I have the worst self-image ever, and I still struggle with it. He made me feel like I was this wonderful person. He made me feel that I was worth something.

Tell me about how your relationship developed after your sophomore year.

Rodney: I went home for the summer and Cathy stayed up here. We only called each other once a week and only talked for twenty minutes.

Cathy: I tend to be dependent on people. I would be like, "Oh Rodney, I need you to be there for me." But because we made that commitment to talk only twenty minutes, I had to make it on my own and depend on God.

That summer was a hard one for me. I visited Rodney for a week, and I wasn't a part of anything about his hometown. It was weird. The friends he grew up with were there, his old girlfriend was there, his house was filled with things that I knew nothing about. He had tons of things that his old girlfriend had made for him. I really struggled with jealousy. I really had to ask myself, "Do I trust him enough, do I actually believe that he really cares for me?" Trust was a really big thing. And there was no middle ground. Either I didn't or I did.

Rodney: Previously Cathy often would go into a relationship for a year and then pull out again. When she would come home on furlough, she would be with somebody for a year and then have to leave. She would shut off her emotions and go back overseas. It was hard for her to say that she was going to stick with this for more than a year. That was a time when we had to really work at our relationship.

It was difficult during our junior year, too. I was

a Resident Advisor. I had to be in the dorm three nights a week and I had a class on another night, so that was four nights out of the week where I couldn't see Cathy. Football would take me away also.

We decided to work on the time we had together, and not whine about the time we didn't have together. Cathy would come over to the dorm and just sit and talk. The guys on the floor loved having her there.

Cathy: We tried not to make them feel like they had to leave so we could be alone. We tried to be open and let them in on our lives. I liked being with the guys, but I had to work on being willing to let Rodney go. I would get frustrated and mad sometimes because I couldn't be with him, yet he could be with all the guys on the floor. I had to be willing not to be selfish and just to accept reality.

I guess you could say we struggled with the physical part of our relationship in our junior year. We were sorting through new emotions. Before that time it was pretty much just friendship. We didn't kiss until we'd known each other for six months.

I had my own apartment and he was in the dorm. We couldn't make out there, so when we were together all our emotions just came out and we'd express it physically.

We both knew that sex was something we wanted to reserve for marriage, so we made that commitment in our sophomore year. I think that makes a difference when you hear yourself say out loud that sex is not an option and you make that commitment to each other. But struggling with other things. . . .

Rodney: . . . like getting together and just kissing and not talking.

Cathy: Which is something that is easy to do because it is so much easier to do. And kissing does show how you care about someone. But sometimes we would make out for longer than we would normally, and we would say, "Wait a minute, what are we doing? This isn't beneficial to our relationship."

Rodney: Then we would try to pull back. We almost got carried away sometimes, though. It didn't help that sometimes we were in the wrong place at the wrong time. Like if there wasn't anybody at her apartment we would say, "We've got to get out of here before something happens." It's too dangerous.

Cathy: This year we've struggled with our physical relationship, too. It's hard when you know you're going to be married, but you definitely don't want to spoil things.

Rodney: In a lot of ways Cathy and I are getting to the point of being one in all ways but physically. It's kind of a frustrating point, because we want to give ourselves to each other physically, but we know we can't so then we get tense inside.

          The summer after our junior year, her parents asked us to come to Africa to work with them. We were in Africa for three months together, and I spent a lot of time with her family. I was able to see Cathy within the context of her own family. I think that was a crucial thing. We could spend time with God every morning separately and then at night we would come together and pray for other people from school who were on mission trips. And it helped us physically as well, because in that culture you would never, ever be physical in public.

Cathy: So we never showed any physical contact for three months. And that's a long time. Our friendship just bloomed, because the physical was less dominant.

We still don't hold hands on campus very much. Just maybe the last couple of months we've been doing that. We had decided we didn't want to do that because it looks so possessive.

Tell me a little about your families and how they enter in your life.

Cathy: My family was the only stabilizing thing I had in my growing-up years because we lived in so many places. We lived in Vietnam, we lived in Europe, and then we went to Africa. With that kind of lifestyle, you are constantly saying good-bye to people. So my family became my closest friends.

Rodney: The first time I visited Cathy's family I felt really accepted, like they cared what I thought. I didn't feel a need not to say certain things. I just said what I thought.

They are a lot more affectionate than my family so it was easier for me to go into her family than it was for her to be with mine. Her parents' respect for people and their love for God really attracted me.

There are ten kids in my family: eight boys and two girls. The two girls are at either end and the boys are in between. We are all very athletic and competitive.

My parents struggle with the fact that I want to go overseas. My parents have a hard time expressing their love verbally, but in showing their love they are incredible. My dad has never missed any activity that his kids were involved in. Three of my brothers were in three different places playing, and we would go to each place for a half hour to see each one play.

But they are just not super affectionate or world-minded. The hardest thing for Cathy when she visited was that they were hospitable, but not in the way Cathy is used to. In my house you are never offered anything to drink, say. I grew up on a farm and if you were thirsty you just went and got yourself a drink. There was never enough food in my family, and you didn't get snacks or help yourself to anything in the cupboard. It was so strange for me when I was with Cathy's family, because they did things so differently. Just a simple thing like having two bowls of cereal for breakfast was different. In my family, we would get one bowl of cereal and never a thought of getting a second one.

Cathy: I find it hard to have a real serious conversation with his parents. I sat down last Christmas and tried to talk to his mother, but she just would not open up. I realize I can't make her be like my mother, so I've just tried to see what I can learn from his family and what he can learn from mine.

How did you two get engaged?

Cathy: My birthday was on September 19th, a Thursday, and Rodney was going to take me into Chicago. The day before I was in Rodney's apartment getting supper for us. I went into his room looking for some money because I had to run to the store. Looking around Rodney's room I found this note that said something about a diamond ring. And I just said, "Gosh." I was in a state of shock. Then I went into his drawer to get some money and I saw two ring boxes in there and I said, "No!" I was starting to freak out. So I pretended I didn't see anything, and I just cooked dinner.

The next night he was going to take me to Chicago. He gave me a dozen roses and I was thinking in my mind, *I'm getting engaged tonight.* My expectations were way up. I wrote in my diary, "I know it's going to happen tonight."

He took me out to dinner and we had a nice time. It was a little uncomfortable because I was anticipating what was going to happen.

We took a carriage ride and he put his arm around me and I could feel this ring box poking me in the side. I was getting really nervous. He said, "Cathy, can I give you your birthday present?" and I said, "Sure." So he took out this box and in it was my pearl ring that he had given me about a year and a half ago. He had gotten it fixed. So he gave it to me and all I could say was, "It's beautiful, Rod." I was expecting a diamond, you know, and he was saying, "Do you like it?" The whole rest of the ride in the carriage I did not say a word. I was really hurt. I think I was also mad.

We cannot hide things from each other, so in the car on the way home I just spilled everything. I said, "Rodney, I'm just so hurt. I thought we were going to get engaged tonight," and so on. I told him about seeing the box in his drawer.

He said he was sorry and I told him I could wait until November, December, or January or whenever to be engaged.

Two days later, we went to a meeting and talked to a lot of people. One girl even checked my ring finger to see if I had gotten engaged. Afterward we went for a walk. He said, "Why don't we go to Northside Park?" I wanted something to drink so we stopped at a 7-Eleven. We were taking it real slow.

At the park we parked the car and he wanted to walk over to this little cabin in the park. As we were walking I saw a flickering light over there. I told him that I thought someone was over there and I didn't want to go. He said, "Let's go see." As we got closer I could see that it was a table with a candlelight dinner set up outside the cabin. I said, "Rodney, someone's eating over there! I'm not going over there." He said, "Well, let's just go over and see who it is."

So he finally gets me about 100 yards from the place and I see a bum sitting under a tree. I said, "Rodney, there's a guy over there!" I was starting to get scared. He told me to just ignore him. So we go over and sit down at this table set with crystal and china, and his roommate Jay comes out from behind the cabin dressed in a tux, ready to wait table for us. I was kind of half shocked, half bewildered, half thrilled. I had no idea of engagement in mind because we had said that would be in the future. I was just set to have a good time. I asked Rodney why he had done this for me and he said he had felt so bad about the other night when I was disappointed.

So Jay took our order. We had filet mignon, twice-baked potatoes, beans, salad, warm rolls, everything! Jay had to go all the way back to the parking lot to get the food out of his car. So we ate the meal and Jay cleared the dishes and then he blew the candle out! Rodney says, "What'd you do that for?" At that point I could tell they were kind of acting, but I didn't know what they were

The Campus Life Guide

up to. Jay said he thought we were done eating. Rodney said, "Well, we want to talk some more. Do you have a match?" Jay said he didn't, so Rodney told him to go ask the bum, who had started to walk away. So Jay went over and asked the guy and the guy took one of those big match boxes out of his pocket and gave it to Jay. He gave it to Rodney and Rodney said to me, "Why don't you light it?" He was acting very natural. I opened one end of the box and there were no matches there. So I opened the other end and there was a ring box! I didn't know what to do. I opened it and just sat staring at this diamond. Then Rodney knelt down and asked me to marry him. It was kind of awkward because I wasn't used to that kind of thing. But I was so excited. He hugged me and shouted, "She said YES!" and some of his friends, who had been hiding in the bushes, let off fireworks and stuff. He hadn't planned that part of it.

We went over to the parking lot and a friend drove up in a BMW and opened the door and told us he's our chauffeur for the evening. We drove around for about an hour drinking sparkling grape drink and listening to romantic music.

It was a fun evening.

Rodney, did you plan on Sunday night all along?

Rodney: Yeah. I knew Cathy was going to expect it so I had to do it at a time that she wouldn't expect. It's hard to fool Cathy.

WHAT DO YOU THINK OF CATHY AND RODNEY?

Maybe you think they are too good to be true. Maybe they are. I didn't spend enough time with them over a long period to really get to know all their quirks. But it seemed to me that they had made the choices we all have to make sooner or later—and to my mind, they made good choices. Let's look at some of those choices now.

WHO COMES FIRST?

When love happens—even the slow, steady love that Cathy and Rodney built up—the tendency is to focus on the other to the exclusion of everyone else—including God. You probably don't have to think too hard to recall someone you know who "fell in love" and left friends and God behind. Or at least relegated them to the sidelines, in the name of their great love.

Rodney and Cathy didn't do this. Both of them had individually made a commitment to follow Christ first, to do whatever he wanted them to do. As their relationship developed, they had to periodically reaffirm, both individually and together, that commitment to put God first.

In fact, it was this spiritual bond that drew them together. Rodney and Cathy had both made decisions to serve the Lord in missions. What freedom to realize that this person is on the same path you are!

Cathy and Rodney consciously kept other friendships alive. They realized the danger of possessiveness, exclusivity. Though it was hard for Cathy to share Rodney with his dorm mates, that became a positive tension in their relationship. It was also probably one of the reasons other people benefited from their relationship.

BUILDING EACH OTHER UP

How do you nurture a friendship? Cathy and Rodney continually found ways to build each other up. They sent each other notes and poems. They called each other on the phone, took long walks. They found creative ways to say, "I care."

What they didn't do was just as important. They didn't depend on physical expressions alone to demonstrate their love. In fact, aware of the temptations, they tried to stay out of situations in which it would be easy to make out for hours on end.

They also said, out loud and to each other, that sex before marriage would not be an option. As Cathy said, there is something powerful about actually saying it out loud, making that commitment together. It's as though you're making a three-fold promise: to yourself, to the other person, and to God. Such a promise is less easily broken, even in the heat of the moment.

Cathy and Rodney weren't afraid to take things slowly; they didn't express their love too quickly. To Cathy, Rodney's "You're the best" meant more than "I love you." She had heard "I love you" before, often in terms of "I love you and I want something from you." Rodney's respect for her as a person nurtured her trust and love more than anything else.

TRUST AND ACCEPTANCE

Trust. It's not always easy to learn. Cathy had more of a problem with it, for she had had more negative experiences. When she visited Rodney and his family and saw all the evidences that Rodney had had another serious relationship before her, she had to choose to trust.

She also had to accept all of Rodney—including his past, and his family which was so different from hers. For Cathy, trust and acceptance didn't just happen; they were choices.

Cathy and Rodney made time to find out about each other's family. They realized that an important part of understanding each other is understanding each other's roots. The fact that their backgrounds were so different made it all the more important to understand and come to appreciate the other's family.

LEARNING FROM EACH OTHER

It seems there's a debate: do opposites attract, or do "birds of a feather flock together"? Well, both. In Rodney and Cathy's case, we see that in some ways, they were opposite: Cathy is open, friendly with almost everyone, very in touch with her feelings. Rodney is more reserved, more rational, less impulsive. I've seen relationships in which such differences grated on the other's nerves. But with Rodney and Cathy, the differences posed an opportunity for growth. I think this is because of how they chose to view the differences.

First of all, they accepted the differences—they did not try to change the other person to become more like them. Second, they appreciated the differences. This opened them up to learning ways to find balance in their own selves. Cathy is learning to become "more logical and accepting of reality." Rodney is learning how to be in touch with his feelings.

In deep ways, they are very similar. And it was the similarities that drew them together: their commitment to overseas work, the importance of family, their agreement on the priority of friendship. Their common values and goals were like glue, holding everything together. Their differences blend together to form a unique picture of one growing relationship.

14. *Dating a Non-Christian?*

Before I became a Christian two years ago, I was dating a guy whom I really liked. After my conversion I told him no more discos, bars, or dancing. He was upset. We argued about salvation. He took me home, dropped me at the curb, and drove off.

I heard from him a month later. He wrote me every month or two, but I put off writing back. Why? Because he's not a Christian. I thought I should not associate with non-Christians.

After a year, I began to write him occasionally, more often during the past two months. I've made dates and have broken them, because I feel it's wrong to date him. I finally told him that I care about him, and made a date for Saturday.

He's fairly open-minded, kind, considerate and gentle. He's expressed an interest in coming to a youth meeting with me. I've asked him if he really understands what I mean when I talk about church. He says not really. I've talked about my Christian life, but he doesn't say much.

I've promised myself that I'll go through with meeting him and discuss my beliefs, and I'll witness to him if the opportunity comes up. I feel I have let him down too many times to say no again. I like him a lot. I want to lead him to God. The only way I can express myself to him satisfactorily is to see him in person.

I know that 2 Corinthians 6:14–18 says we should never yoke ourselves to an unbeliever. But my parents feel, and I do too at times, that no one has the right to judge others. Matthew 7:1 says not to judge lest you be judged. That's what I feel our church is doing in a pious way. But yet the

Bible seems to give us grounds for judgment. This seems contradictory. What do you think?

Good question. The Bible's message in 2 Corinthians 6:14–18 says believers and nonbelievers ought not to be "yoked" together. When two animals are yoked together they can go in only one direction. Marriage qualifies as that kind of relationship, and so it is wrong for believers to marry unbelievers.

But dating isn't the same as marriage. Two people who go out together remain quite free and independent. There is nothing in the Bible explicitly against such a friendship. The Bible teaches us that we ought to be willing to associate with all kinds of people, as Jesus did. (And he got criticized for it.)

The trouble with dating a nonbeliever is that for most people it's not just a friendly association, it's usually Friendship Plus—friendship with greater attachment in mind. It's part of searching for a permanent partner. When that is the case, going out with a nonbeliever is a risk. You're deliberately opening yourself to the possibility of falling in love with someone you can't marry. The result may be great frustration for both of you.

A great many Christians are already somewhat in love with non-Christians. They have become so entangled that they feel it is impossible, or cruel, to suddenly break off. They keep telling themselves that they will never go so far as to marry a nonbeliever. Their standards, they say, are very firm. And they hope and pray and believe that the one they are growing to love will become a Christian, and then their relationship will be "all right."

Sometimes it works that way (though most of the time it doesn't). The following letter gives an example of a time when it did:

I was a senior in high school and a non-Christian. I did believe there was a God and that his Son was Jesus Christ.

But I never accepted him into my heart. I was sitting alone at lunch when a girl came over to sit with me. She was a Christian. Her brother was on the football team with me; he and I hung around together a lot.

She sat with me every day. We talked a lot, and I fell in love with her. I asked her out. She accepted but said I also had to ask her parents. Her parents said if I wanted to date her I had to go to church with them. So I did.

Yes, I had engaged in premarital sex. I probably would have with her, too, except I respected her very much and I was too scared to try anything for fear of losing her. She explained her view on sex. I didn't agree, but I didn't tell her that. Her parents disagreed with our relationship once they knew it was getting serious. I started going to Bible studies and Christian fellowships. Then at a concert a speaker called for people to come down and accept Jesus Christ. I didn't go forward, but in my heart I accepted Jesus Christ as my personal Savior. I have never been happier. I feel a glow inside me I have never felt before.

We are still dating; it's been a year now. I'm in the army and her parents have finally realized they can't break us up, although they have tried hard. If her parents had not allowed her to go out with me or if she had stopped I would not be a Christian today. How do you expect non-Christians to become Christians if you don't date them or become good friends?

This is the advice I would give Christian girls: If a guy does not respect you, he probably never will. If he wants to date you seriously, ask him to go to church with you every Sunday so he doesn't waste your time. It may not help, but it is a start.

ATTRACTIVE, INTELLIGENT, AND CHARMING __

That strikes me as a pretty realistic letter. It presents an unusual case, but it isn't a unique case. A lot of people have become Christians through dating a Christian. But there are also lots who haven't, and their relationships are a sad contrast. Here's an example of the other side:

Last summer, I moved away from the small town I grew up in and came to Ft. Worth. For the first time, I was all alone without my parents to support me. I considered myself a strong Christian who could handle any situation, especially when it came to dating.

Not too long after I moved Keith popped into my life. He was attractive, intelligent and very charming. The only problem was that he was not a Christian. Although I knew it was wrong, I agreed to go out with him.

Eric Liddell once said, "Compromise is the language of the devil." I never realized how true that was until I found myself in bed with Keith only three weeks after our first date. Although I knew our relationship was not pleasing to God, I didn't have the strength to call the whole thing off.

Another month passed and Keith announced that he wanted to break up with me. By that time I had fallen in love with him and his news devastated me. I had hopes of marrying him and having his children. I wanted to hate him but I couldn't.

During the next couple of months I quit eating; I did nothing but work and sleep. I had given Keith something that was so precious to me, and he had used me, then dumped me.

I woke up one day and decided that I couldn't live that way anymore. I reaffirmed my commitment to Christ and accepted his forgiveness. Then I forgave myself and Keith. I got involved in a super church and met some good Christian friends who have helped me through this situation.

I now have a boyfriend who is committed to Christ and loves me the way I need to be loved. God has turned something bad into something good. I still have scars from my ordeal with Keith, but I no longer have to live with guilt. I've learned that God is always willing to give us a second chance no matter how badly we've blown it. I praise him for the second chance he's given me.

You would have a hard time convincing this person that dating a non-Christian is a harmless exercise in friendship. I believe that most people fit into her category. They're hungry for love; their hearts are wide open. Once they take the first step with someone like Keith there's not much chance of turning back. Love is very strong, and once you hand it the controls of your life, it rarely gives them back.

WHAT ABOUT JUDGING? _____

When Jesus told us not to judge, he never meant we weren't to notice what people are like and what they believe. He told us to be as wise as serpents. He himself was a shrewd observer of people, tailoring his message to their needs.

Judging people in the negative sense means writing them off. That's what Jesus spoke against. Some Christians do this by living as if all nonbelievers are immoral and a waste of time to befriend. Such Christians are dead wrong. Jesus warns them that they can be judged by the same standards they have judged by.

But that doesn't mean we shouldn't be wise about the kind of relationships we form with people. I would be slow to entrust my deepest secrets to a gossip, or to lend my VCR to a thief. Most Christians, being wise enough to know themselves and their own weakness for love, do well to never open the door to romantic love with anyone they can't see marrying. Love is too easy to start, and too hard to stop.

One thing worth noting is the advice from the guy who was converted through dating a Christian. What stands out is that he was always afraid of losing his girlfriend. She and her parents communicated, right from the beginning, that they were in control. He would have to walk carefully if he wanted to keep the relationship going. How very opposite that message is from the one that Keith received. Keith must have known from the beginning that he was the one pulling the strings.

Paul, who warned against being "yoked" to unbelievers, knew too well the difference between life in Christ and life without Christ. The difference is not between a good person and a bad one. We are all the same in God's sight. The difference is between a life that has God's light shining on it, and a life in the shadows. For Paul, to go back into the shadows is inconceivable. "What fellowship can light have with darkness? . . . As God has said, 'I will live with them and walk among them, and I will be their God, and they will be my people. Therefore come out from them and be separate,' says the Lord" (2 Corinthians 6:14, 16–17). He didn't mean, "Have nothing to do with them." He meant, "Be different—and don't tie yourself to those who aren't."

15. *Parent Problems*

When I was 14, my best friend already had a boyfriend. One time she wanted to double-date. I felt great—Ray's friend wanted to go out with me! I asked my parents. My father said, "No dating until you're 16."

I stormed into my room and slammed the door. I burst into tears. I saw my social life falling to pieces around my ears. Sixteen! By that time, I'd be so pegged as a "non-dater" that I'd never have a boyfriend. My dad came into my room. "You're ruining my life!" I shrieked at him. My dad didn't know what to do or say. I think he just left me to face my ruin alone.

That was a difficult period, for both me and my parents. I felt their rules were too restrictive, and all I could see was myself losing ground on the social scene. They, I'm sure, saw a lot of other things: statistics on teenage pregnancy, sexually transmitted diseases, etc. I would say to them, "You don't trust me!" They would answer, "We trust you. We just don't trust guys." I didn't like that picture of guys as all sex-crazed animals.

Eventually my parents and I worked out our differences. It was push-pull, push-pull all the way. I was forced to think through my values very carefully. And then, though it was hard to do, I had to communicate what those values were. I had to do it again and again, and I had to live by them to convince them I meant it.

I called myself a Christian, said I believed sex was meant only for marriage. If they were to believe I meant that, I had

"OH, THEN YOU'RE NOT FRENCH? THAT'S ODD... I THOUGHT KATHLEEN SAID SHE HAD A DATE WITH 'THE BIG JACQUES'..."

to also prove I lived by other Christian values. I had to respect them. I had to be loving. I had to prove that I had a mind of my own and was strong enough to stand up to peer pressure on other issues, like drinking and drugs. Eventually they did trust me. By the time I was 17, I didn't even really have a curfew. They trusted my judgment.

That is where most teenagers want to be, in the place where their parents trust their judgment. One 16-year-old girl from Illinois told me, "I wish my parents knew they could trust me. I am probably even more concerned than they are about the high standards I set for myself on a date and the quality of person I am going out with." She speaks for many.

PROBLEM #1: PARENTS ARE TOO STRICT _____

A lot of kids feel that their parents are too strict about dating. Girls especially find that their parents seem to be overly protective. Bridget says, "I'm the only girl in my family, and when I started dating my parents wanted to know if the boy goes to church, how old he is, and why I was going out with him."

Often the conflict is over a rule that just doesn't seem workable, as Joy, a high-school freshman, discovered:

> My problem is my dad won't let me go out with any guy who isn't a Christian. No dances, no plays, no football games. Double dates are suspect too. He and I talked about dating last summer and set down the rules. We said if there was a problem we'd talk about it later.
>
> At that time, dating wasn't much of an issue. I was the tomboyish sidekick, pretty much just one of the guys.
>
> But over the summer I changed physically, spiritually, and socially, and I feel more like a pretty girl. I think that because of my Christianity people are attracted to me. I'm someone they can trust, who is open, always there, mostly happy, and fun to be around. This year in high school I've made many new, good, close friends of both sexes, and I'm attracted to some of the guys. But there's one hindrance: They're not

Christians. And there are no Christian organizations on campus, although I keep pushing for one, and so I really have no way of meeting Christian guys. Nobody from my church even goes to my school.

I find myself disliking my dad and thinking ot rebelling because I think he's being unfair. I realize he wants the best for me, and I appreciate that, but I think I should be allowed to make my own decisions. I believe I have good judgment and am able to tell the good guys from the bad. And I still want to let my dad meet the guy before going out on a date. I would trust his judgment after such a meeting. I just don't understand why I couldn't date a guy who might have the same moral beliefs as I do, just because he isn't a Christian."

Joy's dad has set a limit for her: Don't go out with anyone who doesn't believe as she does. Other parents have other kinds of limits: You can't go out with someone who is of another race, or social status, or who doesn't do as well in school, or whatever. If you agree with the limits, obviously you won't have a problem. But what if you, like Joy, can't see eye to eye with your parents?

First off, you have to try to understand why your parents set their standards. What are they worried about? Joy needs to plan another conference with her dad so she can find out his reasons. Guessing gets no one anywhere. Once she knows why he set that rule, she can work on an appropriate response.

If her dad is thinking about a guy's morals, there's a good chance Joy can convince him to allow her a wider choice. Not all guys (or girls) who call themselves Christians hold to Christian morals, and plenty of non-Christians have excellent moral convictions. The question is: How do you tell? There's no certain way, but Joy can discuss the point with her dad and possibly reach some middle ground. It may be a question of establishing her own moral standards very clearly, and promising her dad she won't go out even once with a guy who doesn't agree with them. Her willingness to let her dad talk to her boyfriends in advance ought to help.

GABBOTT

" ...YOUR PARENTS REALLY ARE STRICT ABOUT YOUR DATING. "

If Joy's dad is thinking ahead to marriage, that's a very different issue, and hard to compromise on. Joy, at 14, probably just wants to go out and have fun. Her dad may see dating differently: as the process of mate-hunting, not fun-hunting. He'd have a point. At 14 dating may just be fun, but in a very few years marriage becomes a real possibility. If non-Christians are part of the process now, they'll more than likely be part of the process later.

Joy's dad may value a marriage between two Christians so much that he considers it OK for Joy to lose a little fun now. Here's where Joy's own spiritual maturity would be tested. If she's honest with herself, she'd have to admit that her dad's perspective certainly fits with the emphasis of the Bible, which warns us, "Do not be yoked together with unbelievers" (1 Corinthians 6:14). We've already looked at the reasons it isn't good for Christians to get into Friendship Plus relationships with nonbelievers: Two people going in opposite directions in life ought not to be "yoked"; they'll just pull and haul on each other.

Suppose Joy's father is basing his reasoning on Scripture, and won't allow any compromise—what can Joy do? What can you do if your parents won't budge on an issue, even after you've talked things over and explained your own position?

What you shouldn't do is rebel, as Joy was considering. That is absolutely a losing proposition. The Bible instructs us to obey our parents, not for their good, but for ours. You may successfully sneak out of the house a few times, but that won't change the basic fact that your parents control your life until you're old enough to leave home. You won't gain freedom; you'll only ruin your relationship with your parents—a serious loss. Our parents probably affect our emotional stability more than any other factor in life. Besides, you usually get caught. And I don't need to tell you what that will do to trust-building.

What you ought to do is seek a creative solution. Maybe your parents won't allow anything but group dating until a certain age. Well, you can still protect and even enhance your popularity by being the one to organize parties. Or maybe your parents set for you what seems to be a ridiculous curfew. All your friends get to stay out till 1 A.M., and you have to be in by eleven. Maybe you can suggest more weekend-afternoon-into-the-evening dates. Or you could see if you could be home by 11, but invite your date in to watch some TV after the curfew.

In Joy's case, the solution would be to find a way to get some Christian guys into her life. She could be the one to start a Christian group on her campus. She could organize trips with people from her church, so that she makes sure they're a more integral part of her life.

Taking the initiative and thinking up creative solutions to your situation will take energy and guts, no doubt about it.

But look at the options: You can sit at home and mope; you can rebel; or you can make the most of the possibilities you have. An added bonus to working within the limits your parents set is that when parents see their kids taking disappointment with maturity, they sometimes loosen up.

PROBLEM #2: MY PARENTS JUST DON'T UNDERSTAND

This often goes hand in hand with Problem #1. But it is also a separate complaint. Sometimes I hear from teenagers whose parents aren't necessarily strict. It's just that they don't provide the support their kids would like.

One girl complained, "I need to see my boyfriend more. I feel my parents don't understand that because they see each other every day." Another said, "My parents didn't understand why it was such a big deal to me that nobody was asking me out. They kept saying, 'Wait until college.' But it really bothered me to think that maybe I wouldn't have a boyfriend before then."

How can this lack of understanding be an obstacle to the Dream? Well, for one thing, our relationship with parents affects the kind of relationships we look for. If we feel secure in their love for us and for each other, we will usually seek out healthy relationships. If there's a breakdown at home, we're more likely to get involved in relationships that feel a lot like love, but aren't healthy. We may not like it, but it's a fact: our parents are very influential people in our lives. We want and need them to understand, to support us, to give us perspective.

Life can get pretty confusing sometimes, as one girl said. She wished her parents understood that, and at the same time understood that "their opinion really does matter." A high-school senior guy admits that even though his parents don't seem to understand, they probably do. "My mom has told me lots of things like, 'If you don't watch out in this situation, you'll get burned,' and I didn't listen to her and I got burned royally."

Maybe you've never thought of it this way, but it gets confusing for parents too. It's hard to see their little boy or little girl grow up. They hear about all the problems facing teenagers today: suicide, drug and alcohol abuse, rampant premarital sex and the resulting problems of disease and pregnancy. And they're scared. They know you need freedom, but they're not sure it's safe. They believe in giving you your privacy, but they don't want to be shut out of your life. Often they seesaw between being reasonable and unreasonable. They really may have forgotten what it was like to be a teenager.

So how do you help them understand? Obviously, not by continually reminding them in frustration, "You just don't understand!" and storming off to your room. If you want them to understand you, you have to take the time to talk to them. The trick here is to find a time when they're not distracted. If they're busy, they're much more likely to give you a pat, hurried answer without really listening. Then you feel you're not heard, and another brick is added to the wall between you.

If you haven't been in the habit of sharing much personal information with them, start small. Share one personal thing with them, how you felt about something that happened in school that day, let's say. It doesn't have to be a deep, personal secret. But if you get in the habit of sharing some of your feelings and opinions with your parents, you may find it easier to receive their support and advice on more personal matters.

Also, volunteer to tell them exactly where you stand on the issues that may secretly worry them. Make it clear what you think about using drugs and alcohol. Tell them how your faith affects who you go out with and what you choose to do on dates. You'll probably find your parents will pry less. (The reason they pry in the first place is to figure out what you think and feel about whatever they think is important.) They may trust you with more freedom.

You can also build understanding by asking them some

144   *The Campus Life Guide*

fun-type questions, helping them remember back to when they were young. For instance: How did you meet? Who asked whom out first? What's the funniest thing that ever happened to you when you were dating? What's the most embarrassing thing that ever happened to you while on a date? How did your own parents react when you first started dating? You—and they—may be surprised to realize that you've been through some similar things.

Teenagers who have good relationships with their parents confirm that it's worth the trouble. If parents see that though they may be losing a child, they're gaining a friend, you're both going to win.

PROBLEM #3: PARENTS ARE TOO NOSY _____

"Parents can be a problem; they can nag you worse than girls," John told me. "What time are you coming home? Who are you going out with? What are you going to do?"

No doubt you relate to his complaint. Sometimes the only communication you feel you have with your parents is the game of Twenty Questions. Why do they nag you so much?

I've already mentioned the answer: They're scared, and they want to be included in your life. Dealing with this problem is relatively easy, provided you're willing to be somewhat open with them. Think through the types of questions they usually ask. Then, tell them your plans before they have to ask. Work on communicating with them about the areas you don't mind them knowing about, and chances are they'll ease up on the Third Degree.

PROBLEM #4: MY PARENTS AND I HAVE DIFFERENT STANDARDS _____

This can take the form of your parents stereotyping your friends by the way they look or dress (which several people told me they hated), to parents not understanding that girls and guys can be just friends, to a parent actually encouraging you to do something you think is immoral (an extreme example, but one I heard about).

Part of growing up is testing your parents' standards, and forming your own. Again, trying to understand your parents' viewpoint and clearly communicating your own is the best approach. If your parents are stereotyping a friend, let them get to know the friend. My parents used to say negative things about some of the guys I hung around with because of the way the guys wore their hair. But after my parents got to know my friends a little better, they loosened up. In fact, they eventually admitted they had misjudged some people. (That was a moment of triumph!) I think they also saw they could trust my judgment.

Most parents will come to respect your values, if they see you have *strong* standards of your own that you *consistently* hold to. The key words are *strong* and *consistently*. They have to see that you're not wishy-washy about your values, and that you live out what you say you believe.

IT ALL BOILS DOWN TO ...

At the heart of most parent conflicts over dating is a mixture of love and fear. Assure them of your love by sharing as much of your life with them as you can. Allay their fears by communicating your standards—by both your words and your actions.

Obviously, in order to successfully communicate to parents that you're trustworthy, you have to have a pretty clear idea of what your standards are. Possibly nothing is more crucial in making sure that you keep the Dream alive. In the next chapter we'll talk about some of the toughest pressures you'll deal with—pressures your parents are all too aware of, pressures that are at the heart of their fears for you.

"CINDY WILL BE DOWN IN A FEW MINUTES. WHY DON'T WE USE THAT TIME TO SEE IF I CAN BUY YOU OFF?"

to Dating

The Campus Life Guide

16. Sex and the Dream

If you turned to this section first, there is good reason. Sex is an integral part of the Dream. God designed sex for two human beings who come together in the middle of a very hostile world to offer their love to each other. In that healing climate, the two are involved in intimacies and expressions of love so private they wouldn't talk to anyone else about them. They share total oneness. They create a small kingdom where the hostilities of the world can't get to them.

Sex is the language of the Dream. Through it these two persons communicate and become one. In this context sex is truly beautiful. Who wouldn't want it? As one high-school girl from Rhode Island put it, "I finally had sex because of *relationship*. I was dying inside and there was no way I was going to lose *relationship* with that other person."

There's one hitch: The Dream is, by definition, a strong, loving, solid, committed, multi-dimensional relationship. The only climate it will thrive in is marriage. (Even there, it takes continuing effort on the part of both people, as the high divorce statistics prove.) Transplant the Dream to any other soil besides marriage, and it will wither.

Not only will your Dream wither, but as a result you as a person will shrivel up inside. It's not that your hair will fall out or you'll get wrinkles early. But something inside of you—your hope to live the Dream—will die.

If there is any one thing that derails people from achieving the Dream, it's letting the Plus side of the relationship get out of hand. Sometimes the damage is felt immediately; sometimes it's more long term. The stories below are just a few of the many true-life examples of how the Dream can be twisted by trying to speak the language of love prematurely.

You know how sex is supposed to bring people closer together? Well, we were closer for about a day, and then I started seeing some changes. We just weren't the same anymore. This wonderful couple that everybody thought would stay together forever was breaking apart—fast. After the second time, Billy wanted to break up. He explained that if we stayed together any longer we would never be able to stop this habit we were beginning to form.

—High-school girl, Texas

I didn't realize how much a wrong relationship could tear away at our relationship with Christ. I'm still feeling the negative spiritual effects of this relationship even after many months. I know the wounds can heal, but I also realize the scars will never go away. I was a strong Christian and thought I could control the relationship. I was wrong, very wrong.

—College guy, Ohio

Having premarital sex was the most horrifying experience of my life. It wasn't at all the emotionally satisfying or the casually taken experience society says it is. Having sex was extremely personal. I felt as if my insides were being exposed and my heart left unattended. Sex is definitely something to be shared with someone who is very gentle, very caring, and who will also be personal with you for the rest of your life.

—College girl, Virginia

My boyfriend and I both attended a Christian high school, and we knew premarital sex was wrong. But we loved each other, and felt sex only deepened our relationship. Many times we tried to quit but our resolve never lasted, and our relationship got . . . stronger? Well, maybe, if stronger means his demands on me increased to have sex in the worst places, with less and less consideration of my feelings.

But when our relationship became rocky, and he wanted to break up, I couldn't bear the thought of my boyfriend being shared with someone else.

Well, we stuck it out for four years, and when I was 18, and he was 19, we married. We never fought or argued (the only thing we argued over before was sex), just lived together without guilt, but also without respect for each other's feelings. We had lost that years ago. And sex was no big deal because that sacredness was thrown out the window.

Did you ever eat too much cookie dough and when the cookies are baked, you don't want any?

After one year of marriage, my husband left me and moved in with a girl he worked with. It wasn't until then—until I sat alone, rejected, pregnant, and burned by the fire I had kindled—that I finally understood why the Bible says to wait. Why would a man (or woman) honor God by keeping a marriage covenant when we couldn't honor him (and each other) before marriage? We surely reap what we sow.

These true experiences from young people—and I could add many more—remind me that God was not trying to deprive us when he told us to keep sex within marriage alone. Remember, he was the one who created this powerful thing called sex. He wants us to enjoy it. He put the outline of the Dream in each of our hearts, and he gives us the freedom to fill in that outline with colors and shapes and patterns unique to us.

At the heart of the Dream is a relationship called Friendship Plus. Friendship based on mutual respect, concern, shared values, and a shared faith, Plus the spark of romance and sexual attraction. They are two sides of true love, and they shouldn't be confused. As one college guy from Texas said, "Too often love and sex are confused. Granted, they should go together, but they are not synonymous." If we focus on Friendship-love and let Plus-love take a back seat, we're on the road to the Dream. But, as I already pointed out, we shouldn't (and can't) ignore the Plus completely. And here is where we have a huge challenge.

THE PROBLEM WITH SEX

"Plus" doesn't even mean the same thing to guys and girls. Chalk it up to social learning or biology (nobody knows for sure), the fact is that girls and guys respond to sex differently. For a guy, the sex trigger tends to be the eye or the mind's eye—what he sees or imagines. "Plus" means sexual attraction. For a girl, the Plus is more tied to romance. Her sex trigger is often a caress, a touch, or even deep feelings about love, security, home, and family.

One big reason problems develop when guys and girls go out is they don't understand how their partner reacts. A girl, not understanding a guy's struggles with his urges, will often dress provocatively on a date. She doesn't necessarily understand that it's provocative; maybe it's just the style. But whether she realizes it or not, it starts the guy's motor running as soon as he sees her.

So right from the start, the guy is building up steam in his tank. His imagination is working. The girl doesn't even realize it: She's thinking about where they're going, how much the food is going to cost, how much she dares order.

Then later, after the date, they go someplace and begin to make out. She begins to get a few bubbles rising in her tank, too. He's already got quite a head of steam.

Somebody said boys will give love to get sex; girls will give sex to get love. One college guy from Tennessee admitted, "On several different occasions I found myself telling my partner that I loved her when in all honesty I was really more in love with how she was making me feel." And a high-school girl said, "All I know is that Bobby offered me something that no one else had offered: He was a friend. For the 'small' price of giving him my body, he would listen to me, hold me, and let me cry on his shoulder. He cared—or at least he acted like he cared—and at that point in my life, that's all that was important."

Too often we think we have to trade sex for love, or that the only way to express love or prove love is through sex. But sex muddies the waters of love considerably. One high-school guy put it succinctly when he said, "Sex in dating is a power play; guy pressures girl or girl manipulates guy to get what he or she wants." Love is complicated enough without the issues of power that sex adds.

Sexual attraction is like fire. Out of control, it can burn, even destroy you. Under control, it can warm you and give your love a special glow. If you "let nature take its course"— if you let sex control you—it will rage out of control. If you control it, take the responsibility for making it your servant and not your master, you will reap its benefits in all the years to come.

But just how do you manage something that often seems so powerful?

SEX UNDER THE DREAM

One of the best ways to make sure that sex serves the Dream is to get a clear handle on your own Dream. Write it out for yourself. Think about it often.

A college girl from Illinois applied that this way: "One thing that has helped me is to pray for my future husband every night, even though I have no idea who he is. I pray that he will grow strong in the Lord, strive to do his will, have a strong desire to obey him in every situation, and that he will always love the Lord more than he loves me. The more I pray for him, the more special he becomes. The more special he becomes to me, the more I want to save myself for him. This can help in tempting situations."

You actually free yourself from a tremendous amount of pressure if you set some boundaries for yourself. This goes for both guys and girls. I know a lot of guys live by the rule, "Go as far as the girl will let you." But that doesn't make it right. If you're a guy, you don't have to give in to your hormones like some boar. Claim your humanity, and control your physical impulses.

May I get real specific and offer some practical suggestions? I think it's wise for a guy to make a vow that he will not unzip, unbutton, unsnap, or unhook any part of a girl's clothing. And I think it's also wise for him to make a vow that he won't fondle her body.

And I say this to girls: You should make a vow that you won't allow a guy to do any of those things.

Why do I say this? The dangers I see are really a twofold problem.

The first problem is that as we fondle and touch parts of the body, we begin breaking down inhibitions, which then leads to further intimacy. We never move down the scale of intensity, we always move up it; we always go from less intense situations to more intense situations.

For example, a couple doesn't go from kissing to holding hands. It's the other way around. They go from holding hands to kissing, from kissing to necking, from necking to petting, from petting to intercourse. And the momentum gets stronger at each step; the further you go, the more difficult it is to stop.

The second problem is one of frustration. If you've decided you're not going to engage in sexual intercourse, the further you go, the more frustration (emotionally and physically) you're going to feel. Sometimes that frustration itself is enough to make you charge right on past the limits you've set.

I should add that even if you go all the way, you're very likely to experience another kind of frustration. Your frustration will be that you have to have sex in the strangest, most awkward, and unromantic places—in backseats of cars, under bushes, in rooms where there is always some chance you'll be discovered.

I've met lots of teenagers who thought that they were getting experience for marriage by their premarital sex. But they got almost none, because sex in bucket seats at a drive-in movie and sex in a loving, caring, committed marriage relationship are two very different matters. The second is not only less frustrating, it's more wonderful because it's what God meant it to be.

Deciding on your limits will free you. A high-school girl

154

from Pennsylvania pointed out, "If the stopping point has already been decided, there doesn't even have to be a choice. Sex is simply out of the question. The option is not there, because the decision has already been made."

But once you make the decision, you have to communicate it—clearly. A college girl advises, "The best way to avoid most of the pressure is to get what you believe out in the open. Do not wait. When you and a guy start dating, let him know how you feel about sex. That way he has no excuse later on and he cannot say that you led him to believe this and that. If you get your standards out in the open, there will be no question in anyone's mind."

This can be a little tricky. Obviously, on the first date you don't hit your date with, "By the way, I intend to be a virgin when I get married, so don't try anything." But as it becomes clear that you are developing a Friendship Plus relationship, you need to bring up your standards and make sure they are compatible with your partner's.

I've already talked about putting most of your time and energy into developing the Friendship part of the relationship. That means talking together—a lot, about a lot of things. Remember that a relationship never stands still; it either grows stronger or it begins to fade. Sex may seem to be the easiest medicine for a fading relationship, but it usually only makes matters worse. Sex definitely adds interest, and it seems to communicate deep love. But it won't strengthen a relationship.

KEEPING YOUR RELATIONSHIP ON TRACK _____

If you want to build a strong relationship, ask yourself: What new understanding have we reached in the past few weeks? When did we last have a great conversation? When did we last do something really fun which we had never done before? What new ways of expressing our love and appreciation for each other have we tried lately? Are we growing? Or are we standing still?

Limit the amount of time you spend kissing and hugging.

You can't kiss and have a good talk at the same time. Kissing is not creative communication, no matter how creative it feels. Kissing tends to take over and in time your relationship suffers. Kissing only expresses the love that's come into being; it doesn't strengthen a relationship one bit.

A relationship dominated by physical interaction will be under intense pressure to go further and further. Our bodies work that way. What thrills you one day just gets you hot and sweaty the next. Your body wants to go on, to go all the way. And your body will get its way if you let it. But your mind can and should have the final say. Discuss (preferably in a public place where you're not tempted by the natural heat the discussion produces) exactly what kind of touching is proper and helpful to your relationship. Discuss not only how far you will allow yourselves to go in expressing your love, but decide together on where you will not go, the things you will not do. Talk not only about how far you will go, but for how long: Set time limits. Make decisions now, and then enforce them with each other. Keep your word. Don't review the decisions every weekend—make them and stick by them.

My advice is to set pretty tough limitations on yourselves. It's much easier to stop early than to stop late. And it's usually better for the relationship. I've never known a couple who broke up because they didn't go far enough. I've known many who broke up because sexual attraction eventually dominated their relationship.

Finally, I suggest you spend a good deal of your time together with Christian friends. I know that doesn't satisfy your romantic spirit, which wants to get off alone and look at the moon. It does, however, help to keep your relationship more realistic. You're less prone to be in love with love, and more prone to get to know who the other person really is. You can fool yourselves when you're all alone. Everything looks good bathed in moonlight. But in public you see more clearly. If you can't stand to be together with other people around, then you are a couple with a poor future.

The Campus Life Guide

SOME QUESTIONS

Here's a list of questions to ask yourself if you really want to resist temptation:

1. Is your relationship growing, or has it stalled?
2. Do you communicate well? Are you finding creative ways to express your care for each other (flowers, gifts, poems, songs)?
3. Do you have mutually agreed-upon limits?
4. Are your limits tough enough to "nip temptation in the bud"? Or do you let things almost get out of hand, and then stop?
5. Do you make careful plans in advance for how to spend your time together?
6. Do you spend all your time alone, or are others part of your relationship?
7. Do you both know why you want to resist temptation? Do you have a strong sense of the goodness of sex within marriage, as God designed it? Are you looking forward to the future God has in mind for you?

This list may help, but in the final analysis you and your partner are the ones who must decide what you want to do; you must take control of your lives. It's not an impossible battle you're fighting. Sex is a strong force, but you are stronger.

GETTING BACK ON TRACK

But perhaps you've already made mistakes. Perhaps you know from experience how strong a temptation sex is, and how easy it is to give in. Perhaps you're wondering, "Can the Dream still come true for me?"

The answer is, yes, if you're willing to take some strong action.

You probably feel guilty. Maybe you're wondering, as one girl did, "How can I feel that I have been washed clean of this sin and become close to God again, and not yield to this temptation anymore? I want to know for a fact, without a shadow of a doubt, that God has forgiven me, and I want to feel better about myself again."

There is some good news: God promises forgiveness. The Bible tells us that "If we claim to be without sin, we deceive ourselves and the truth is not in us. If we confess our sins, he is faithful and just and will forgive us our sins and purify us from all unrighteousness" (1 John 1:8–9). Spiritually, it is possible to start all over again. That doesn't mean you forget all the physical and emotional consequences of your past. If someone is pregnant, she has to deal with that. If someone is emotionally troubled, he requires healing. If memories have been created, you can't pretend they're gone.

Spiritually though, you can become a new person. The past is not destroyed, but transformed. You get a second chance, and that means there are no limitations on what you can become. The God who made the universe out of nothing can take the raw material of your past and make from it something beautiful.

So how do you begin such a transformation? You can't manage it on your own. You need God's power. And where do you find that? You ask for it. Spiritual transformation begins as simply and as mysteriously as that. You ask, admitting your need. And God goes to work in your life.

If you've done that—if you've agreed with God that you have sinned and you need his help to keep from sinning— you are forgiven. Totally. God says, "I will forgive their wickedness and will remember their sins no more" (Hebrews 8:12). Again, the Bible says, "As far as the east is from the west, so far has he removed our transgressions from us" (Psalm 103:12).

You may not feel forgiven. Often that takes time. The sense of guilt won't usually change immediately, even though the objective fact is that God no longer considers you guilty. Like other natural consequences—pregnancy, for example—feelings don't necessarily change when God transforms your life. But their sting is taken away.

Jesus did not die on the cross to take away your feelings. He died to take away your sins. Cleansed of sin, you can work on transforming your feelings into a useful tool for God's service. Transformed, they can give you compassion for the pain of other people. They can give you deep determination not to go wrong again. And you'll need that determination, because you will have to work even harder at reclaiming the Dream for yourself.

WHAT TO DO

If you've already fallen to sexual temptation, you know from personal experience that there is a law of sex built into our bodies that urges us on. Once you've reached a certain level of intimacy, it's extremely difficult to go back. And this same law draws couples who've already had sexual intercourse to have it again and again—even if they're determined to stop.

This law is good news for those living the Dream, by the way. It's like a magnet, pulling married couples together. But if you're not ready for that kind of commitment, if your love hasn't grown to the point of "going all the way" and yet you've gone "all the way," with your body, you and your partner have a problem. Making a new beginning is doubly difficult. You have to fight off the laws of sex—something like fighting off gravity.

Once you've made sex the center of your relationship, it's hard to take that center away. No matter how much you want to. No matter how truly forgiven you are by God.

You can't fight gravity without some equipment—a set of wings and a motor. You can't fight sexual gravity, either, without some structural help.

Very often, when you go too far the only way to regain control is to cut out all physical contact. Usually that means breaking up. But if two people are in love and genuinely want to quit, with God's help it's sometimes possible to start over without breaking up. Generally this means:

1. A lengthy cooling-off period. How long? Let's say, for starters, two months.

2. Help from an outsider. Find a sympathetic Christian who will pray for you and hold you accountable for your behavior.

3. Try going out on your first date all over again, and get it right this time. If you think all a couple should do on their first five dates is to hold hands, do that and no more. You can't back up just one step in sexual intimacy. If you want to quit sexual involvement you have to go all the way back to the beginning.

It will feel disagreeable and unnatural. It seems so awkward, so childish. Only those with lots of determination put up with it. But it might help to remind yourselves what "feeling natural" did for your relationship.

4. Take the time to talk at length about "getting physical" and what your plan will be as you start over. Talk honestly about what leads up to temptation for you two (for example, lengthy periods alone in each other's homes). Usually temptation doesn't come out of nowhere; there's a whole train of events that precedes it. Trying to stop the train after it's gained speed won't work. You need to stop it before it accelerates.

Can this strategy work? It really depends on how much both people want it to work. Relearning these patterns can feel very frustrating. Is your relationship worth it? You'll have to decide for yourselves.

The following story illustrates how God worked with one couple who wanted to turn their relationship around.

I was a four-month-old Christian at 16 when I met a kind-hearted, 21-year-old guy named Al. Our friendship blossomed into a steady relationship of love and deep commitment. Unfortunately, we began to desire more than just a "good-night" kiss. We began what I guess you would call "light petting." Often we felt guilty afterward and asked for forgiveness. But we fell again and again. It felt so right.

I remember hearing that 99 times out of 100 petting is not good for a couple's relationship. I was so sure that Al and I were the 100th couple. Sometimes we reasoned that something as beautiful as expressing love through petting must be a gift of God, and we even prayed and thanked him for it. And we were right. Petting is a gift from God. Unfortunately we opened it without reading the tag that said, "Do Not Open Until Wedding Day." A wedding day seemed so far off, since I planned to go to college after I graduated. And so the struggle became more difficult as our love grew deeper.

We finally came to the conclusion that we had something that was not rightfully ours, and began to pray for forgiveness. We still fell, and prayed, and fell, and prayed. We knew God wanted us together and so were engaged to be married in 20 months. (Long months.) After the first year of our engagement we still fought physical desires, falling and praying.

Then suddenly it stopped. God seemed to say, "Hey, kids, I want you together, but we need to work hard on our spiritual relationship, and on deepening your friendship and agape love for each other. We've only got seven months, so you'd better quit trying to build your physical relationship. I'll take care of that when it's time. And hey, I really forgive you!"

You'd think that during the last seven months before our wedding we would find it infinitely harder to control our desires than during the preceding two and a half years of dating and engagement. After all, our love and commitment had grown tremendously. But during that period Al and I never even shared a passionate kiss (as opposed to a "good-night" kiss). And because Jesus strengthened us, I can even say it wasn't that hard. We gave up the struggle to Jesus and began learning more about his love by reading his Word and praying nightly before Al went home. I felt as though our engagement really only lasted for those last seven months, because that was the time we were truly being prepared for marriage.

Al and I have been married for over a year now, and we are inexpressibly happy. I do not doubt that we probably lost some of the very first newlywed experiences that God had intended for us. But we also shared and learned much about each other in innocent privacy during those precious first days and nights. And we can still share and learn in this special, exciting marriage love, because we were able to pursue our top priority—our relationship to God—during our engagement.

God can heal, God can strengthen, God can rekindle the Dream in us. I think the right attitude toward sex should be one of excited anticipation. That attitude is eloquently expressed by a college girl from Kansas: "I'm looking forward to having sex. But I want to be a virgin on my wedding night and go through all the excitement, vulnerability and uneasiness of being united with my husband physically. I am so glad that I will not have someone else to compare my husband to and that I can totally concentrate on him and his happiness."

17. *When the Dream Becomes a Nightmare*

Given the fact that everyone has the outline of the Dream inside, you'd think guys would know how to treat girls. And girls would know how to treat guys. That honesty, kindness, and respect would mean something. That people could find their way to selflessness and genuine caring.

Often they do, of course. But that's not always the case. It wasn't for Sandy.

SANDY'S STORY*

Sandy's parents were out of town, so she was spending the night with her friend Julie who lives across from the high school. They made a plan to sneak out and meet their boyfriends at school after midnight. Sandy felt hesitant about sneaking out, but it seemed exciting and she had never done it before.

Being with the guys was fun—meeting secretly, horsing around, kissing a little. After a while Julie got nervous and said it was time to go home. But Sandy wanted to stay a bit longer with her boyfriend, John. Julie went home by herself.

When Sandy decided to go in she tapped on the bedroom window, but couldn't wake Julie. She thought knocking at the door would wake Julie's parents, and she didn't want to get Julie or herself in trouble. Then her boyfriend, John, said, "Why don't you go to your house? I know your parents aren't home, but you have a key, don't you? I'll walk you home, 'cause it wouldn't be safe for you alone at night."

When they got to Sandy's house, she told John good-night

and that she'd talk to him tomorrow. "Couldn't I come in just for a minute, just to rest? I still have a long walk home, you know," John said.

Sandy thought he was nice to bring her home, but didn't want to let him in when her parents weren't there. She was feeling pressured. She said, "No, I'm sorry. You'll have to leave."

He continued to pressure her. "What's the matter, don't you trust me? Couldn't I come in and just get a drink of water?"

Sandy was feeling confused. How could she tell him she was not sure she trusted him? She didn't want to hurt his feelings. He was so nice to walk her all the way home just so she would be safe. How could she refuse him a drink? "OK, you can come in just for a minute, just to get a drink."

They talked for a little longer. John didn't try anything, but Sandy still felt uncomfortable. "You had better go now," she said.

"Only after a kiss," he replied.

Oh no, Sandy thought, *I'll never get him out of the house. He won't listen to me.* "Just one kiss," she said, "then will you go?"

But when she kissed him, he wouldn't let go and that is when it happened: He pushed her down on the couch. She struggled, but John was a lot bigger and stronger. She was on her back, pinned down. Sandy couldn't believe this was happening to her. She thought about reaching for the huge ashtray on the coffee table and hitting him over the head. She thought, *What if I split open his head? What if it makes him so angry that he hurts me worse? What if I knock him unconscious? Whom would I call? What would I say?* "Help, I just hurt this guy I know. I let him into my house when my parents weren't home. I sneaked out with him from my friend's house in the middle of the night and he tried to rape me"? *Who would believe that?*

Sandy fought hard, but John had her pinned down. Trapped.

John thought it was a great date and he was feeling good about himself. He scored.

He'd needed to prove himself, prove he could make a conquest. He was thinking only about himself.

Sandy couldn't believe what had happened. She felt terrible.

Sandy was raped.

IT IS RAPE—EVEN IF YOU KNOW THE GUY _____

Date. Rape. The two words hardly seem to go together. But often they do.

Perhaps you have the idea—many people do—that rape is something that happens only to hitchhikers or late-night streetwalkers. And only by strangers. You may be surprised by this, but date rape is more common than rape by a stranger. As many as 75 percent of all rapes are committed by acquaintances. An alarming number of those are by dates.

What makes rape "rape"? The use of force.

Most of us have heard that rape is primarily a crime of violence, not "sex." But date rape may not seem violent, especially at first. Instead, it may start as "bargaining." Words that one person uses to make another feel pressured into sexual activity. Physical use of force—grabbing, shoving—may follow verbal pressure. But if this is sexual activity that you do not want, that you do not consent to, that you are pressured or forced into, it is rape.

Even if you know the guy.

Even if you have dated for a long time.

Even if you have let him touch you in intimate ways.

Even if you are drunk.

Even if you had sex with him before.

Even if he uses the dumb line that he is "too turned on to stop."

It is still rape.

Laws differ from state to state. It may be difficult to criminally prosecute a person who pressures you into sexual activity but does not use physical force. Some people make a distinction between "sexual exploitation" (taking advantage of, or manipulating a person into sexual activities) and "rape" (physically, violently forcing sexual activity). But the only difference is in how much and what kind of force is used.

If you have been forced into sexual contact with someone, don't hesitate to call it what it is: rape. You may feel confused. Perhaps you gave in out of guilt or fear or even confusion. But this is not the same as consent.

It is still rape.

WHY DOES IT HAPPEN?**

It's confusing. You try to imagine who might take advantage of you sexually, and you think of some drunken bum on a park bench. But the facts show it is more likely someone you know. At least casually. It is probably someone your age or in his 20s or 30s. Sex offenders are not usually the obvious crazies either. They may be loners with few friends, but not necessarily. They are usually normal looking. They may even be intelligent people. Popular people. Religious people.

Date rape is a bit different from rape by a stranger. But there are similarities, too. The person who takes advantage is meeting his own "needs" at the expense of another person. He is not taking responsibility for the harm he is inflicting; he's too wrapped up in himself. He may even dismiss the seriousness of what he's doing with a string of flimsy excuses. Or by passing blame to the person he has wronged. You hear of guys tossing around stupid phrases like this:

"Hey, everybody does it."

"She asked for it. Did you see how she was dressed?"

"She loved it."

"What's the big deal? I didn't hurt her."

Such thin rationalization does not change the fact: Sex without consent is rape.

Why does date rape happen, then? It happens because someone is playing a power game. Is using manipulation or force to get what he wants at your expense.

But date rape is a bit more involved than that.

The offender may like to think of himself as a domineering, macho type. Most sexual offenders do. But so do many guys. And here's where date rape gets more confusing.

Society has certain understood ways of doing things. We think of girls as acting a particular way. Of guys acting a particular way. These understood ways of doing things are called "sex roles." They are ideas—unwritten rules—floating around society. We learn them. Pick them up subconsciously. TV shows them. Movies scream them. Some of them are wrong.

These unwritten rules tell guys: Push for sex; you must make the moves.

The same rules tell girls: Resist, even if you don't really want to. Resist first. Give in maybe later.

These unwritten rules also tell guys: Be tough. They never tell a guy that he ought to be tender, sensitive, respectful. But the rules tell girls: Be passive, sweet, submissive. Don't state clearly what you want. Or don't want.

Such pervasive attitudes on sex help explain why date rape is a unique problem. You have a guy who is reluctant to rein in his hormones anyway. And he understands from society that the rules of the road go something like this: Push for what you want. Be the aggressive initiator. If she resists that doesn't necessarily mean she doesn't want what you are eager to deliver. She may fight and fuss and tease you with a negative response, but persevere. You'll wear down her resistance and eventually get what you want.

"No" doesn't necessarily mean "No!"

And let's face it: Sexual things are not enjoyed only by guys. A girl might, on the one hand, be enjoying some sexual activity, while on the other hand she's struggling to hang on to her limits. The signals she sends may be confusing. And, of course, there are also girls who try to manipulate guys into sex.

As a couple, it's important to put away society's unwritten

rules. To talk about your own limits. To decide on them, when you're not in the heat of the moment. To state them clearly. And to agree that anytime you choose to say No, you can. It's your right. And agree together that No will always mean No!

Don't play games.

This word to guys: The unwritten rules are no excuse. The heat of the moment is no excuse. There is no substitute for simple kindness and respect.

And sex without consent is still rape.

PROTECTING YOURSELF*

There is no perfect way to protect yourself from date rape, but the following guidelines have worked for many people.

1. Know that you have the right to set sexual limits. You may have different limits with different people; your limits may change. It's a good idea to know what you want or don't want before you end up in the backseat of a car.

2. Communicate those limits. Get them across to the other person. Clearly, ESP does not work.

3. Trust your feelings. If you feel you are being pressured into any unwanted physical activity, you are right.

4. Pay attention to behavior that doesn't seem right:

Someone sitting or standing too close who enjoys your discomfort.

Power stares—looking through you or down at you.

Someone who blocks your way.

Someone speaking in a way or acting as if he knows you more intimately than he does.

Someone who grabs or pushes you to get his way.

Someone who doesn't listen or disregards what you are saying (like when you say no!).

5. Be assertive. It's OK to get angry when someone does something to you that you don't want. Act immediately with some kind of negative response.

Stand up for yourself. It's OK to be "rude" to someone who is sexually pressuring you, even if it hurts his feelings. After all, he's not paying attention to your feelings. And if you aren't and he isn't, guess who's going to get hurt? You have every right to protect yourself.

OTHER FORMS OF ABUSE**

Date rape is an extreme form of abuse. Unfortunately, it isn't the only form. The Dream can also be twisted by jealousy, control, fear, and violence. As Nancy discovered.

"I was trying to break up with him. He said, 'You'll never get away from me,' and started choking me. I tried to fight him off. There was lots of yelling. Other people heard it. Then there's a blank. I'm not sure what happened. I think someone came in. He was removed—strapped to a stretcher. It happened in the dorm. How embarrassing."

Nancy (not her real name) is 30 years old now. She still has nightmares of the abuse she endured during a six-year relationship that began when she was 16.

Besides being choked, Nancy was pushed, hit, kicked, threatened with a weapon, and had things thrown at her. She admits to hitting, slapping, and punching her boyfriend "in self-defense. Every time he hit me, I hit him back."

Sound bizarre? Hardly the kind of thing you'd expect to see every day. But problems of abuse are far more common than you might think. Date abuse occurs in as many as 50 percent of all relationships. Most of the victims are female although males are also abused. The abuse inflicted on the men, however, is generally in retaliation for abuse they give out.

While you would naturally think of physically violent behavior as abusive, date abuse is complex, and happens on other levels. There are really four types of date abuse: emotional, verbal, physical, and sexual.

Emotional abuse can be subtle: Withholding affection, giving the silent treatment, failing to fulfill a promise, and ignoring someone are all forms of emotional abuse.

An 18-year-old woman said, "He frequently goes back on promises. I get frustrated with him, and if I say something about it he gets angry."

Verbal abuse is often linked to emotional abuse.

According to Nancy, "He always used to tell me I wasn't attractive enough to get anyone else; I could never live on my own; I'd never make it. I learned not to tell him things—they'd just come back at me. He knew what would hurt me verbally and emotionally. Then he'd use it."

Physical abuse is any unwanted and hurtful physical act. Initially there may be pushes, shoves, or light slaps on the face or other part of the body. Each incident doesn't seem too severe by itself and may go unnoticed for a while.

But when ignored, problems may quickly become severe. Slaps may become punches and hits become beatings, often leaving tell-tale bruises and other marks.

What then follow are violent acts leading to broken bones and internal injuries. Fractured ribs, broken jaws and nose, and concussions are extremely common. As violence progresses, wounds may leave permanent damage such as hearing loss, scars, vision problems, and impaired organ functions.

Homicide is the ultimate act of physical abuse. Although there are no statistics concerning dating homicides, one-fourth of all homicides occur between spouses. This may seem absurd to you now; but such a pattern could easily begin in a dating relationship and needs to be stopped at the first signs of abuse.

Sexual abuse is any sexual contact that is unwanted. It may be subtle—an unwanted kiss or fondle—or extreme, as in rape.

WHY DOES IT HAPPEN?**

Jealousy and the need to control are often a part of the underlying emotions involved in date abuse.

"The abuse started when he was jealous because of my being with my other friends," said one teenager.

The meaning of the boyfriend's response often gets muddled in your mind. You may translate it into: "If he didn't love me, he wouldn't get so angry. And if he didn't get so angry, he wouldn't hurt me." As many as one-third of all teens involved in abusive relationships remain in those relationships even after the violence.

Surprisingly, abuse in relationships is viewed as normal by many young people. In a nationwide survey of 3000 teenagers, one-third of the young men and one-fourth of the young women accept abuse under some circumstances.

Why such widespread acceptance of abuse? While there is no one answer, there are some factors which may partially explain it.

Social acceptance of violence against women. Sadomasochism, rape, and sexual torture are depicted in violent pornography as a man's right and a woman's pleasure. And in one study, 57 percent of college men indicated that they were likely to commit a rape if there were no chance of getting caught.

Sex-role stereotyping. Men who accept abuse as normal in relationships tend to be more sexist in their attitudes about women. Their view of women is very limited. They expect them simply to have babies, take care of the house, and not hold a job outside the home. This may be interpreted to mean: Women exist solely to serve men.

Glorification of violence. Violence on television has increased 65 percent since 1980. The U.S. Attorney General's Task Force on Family Violence reports that the evidence is overwhelming: Television and movie violence play an important role in causing family violence.

Violence is found in 46 percent of all music videos. Almost half of these contain violence between men and women.

Violent role models. At least one million children are abused by their parents each year. About 60 percent of abusive men had fathers who abused their mothers.

WARNING SIGNS**

Can a girl predict if her boyfriend will become physically or verbally abusive? The following warning signs often signal potential abuse. If any of these sound familiar, you're on a course that can destroy your chances of achieving the Dream.

Emotional or verbal abuse can be a signal. Put-downs, name calling, ignoring, and withholding of affection can be the first signs of a guy's inability to cope in an intimate relationship.

Taking control—such as pressuring a girl to stop seeing certain friends, demanding that she dress or act a specific way. Such demands could lead to isolation and extreme dependency on the boyfriend. "Being with my other friends is what got him so angry. He said that they're the wrong crowd for me," said a 17-year-old. This is not a boyfriend's right or place.

Excessive jealousy, which leads to unwarranted suspicion and mistrust, is very common in many abusive relationships. A poor self-image is a characteristic of an abusive male. He may think that his masculinity has been threatened if he sees his girlfriend talking to another guy. "He refused to believe me and there was nothing I could do to convince him that I wasn't flirting," said a teenager who eventually was hit several times by her boyfriend.

Heavy drinking or drug use can contribute to abuse. Sixty percent of abusers are under the influence of drugs or alcohol. These substances may not cause violence, but they often become an excuse for violent behavior.

Childhood violence may have set an example. If the guy has seen his father abuse his mother or if he was abused as a child, he may have more of a tendency to repeat the pattern.

An inability to handle frustrations in normal everyday situations could signal potential violence. If relatively minor situations, such as being jostled in a crowd or late for a movie, cause a guy to blow his top, he probably will not be able to handle the normal frustrations of a relationship.

A guy who frequently punches walls, breaks objects, or throws things in rage could turn on someone close to him. One young woman remembered, "His temper always scared me, but I never thought he'd hit me. I was wrong."

Cruelty to animals indicates a lack of respect for living things. Savagely beating a dog or terrorizing an animal should not be minimized.

IF YOU'VE BEEN ABUSED*

If you've been the victim of physical or sexual abuse, keep in mind the following points:

First, remember your rights. Assault and battery are a crime. A boyfriend has no more right to assault a girlfriend than does a stranger. He can be prosecuted.

Second, there is never an excuse for abuse. A boyfriend might not like something that was said or done and he may become angry, but that does not give license to abuse.

Third, getting hit, pushed, shoved, or abused in any way is not a sign of love. It is a sign that the guy has a problem controlling his anger. Often he will try to blame the girl for inciting him to uncontrollable rage; the girl must not accept the responsibility for the abuse.

Fourth, studies have shown that over time, abuse increases both in frequency and severity. Promises of "I'll never do it again" aren't enough. The abuser must get outside help for his problem or it will continue.

Fifth, talking to parents, friends, or workers in battered women centers can help to deal with the embarrassment, anger, confusion, and fears that accompany being abused.

"LOVING" TOO MUCH

Perhaps it's inconceivable to you that people would let themselves get into these kinds of situations. *Why not just break up?* you may wonder.

On the other hand, maybe you know someone who's being abused. Or maybe your own Dream has turned into a nightmare. And you're wondering, *How does it happen?*

It happens because, unfortunately, not many people in this society have an understanding of what real love is. Listen to our songs: "I want to know what love is . . . I can't live, with or without you . . . I'm addicted to love . . . I can't live, if living is without you . . ." Such songs continually underscore the common idea that when you truly love someone, you can't live without that person.

But that isn't healthy love. It's dependent love. And it's the kind of "love" which sets the stage for the Dream to become a nightmare. It's the kind of "love" that keeps people shackled to relationships that are making them miserable, yet they think they can't get out. Like someone I know, whom I'll call Monica.

Monica is 18, newly married. She often complains about her husband: "He won't let me work, though I've always dreamed about becoming a nurse. He never listens to what I say, or cares about my feelings. And he never talks about his own feelings. He expects me to do all the laundry and cooking, and he never helps." She'll go on and on about how miserable her husband is making her. Then, as if she finally hears how she sounds, she'll switch gears. "But sometimes we get along great. He can be so nice. I love him. I can't live without him. I'm probably making too much out of his faults. Everyone has faults, right?"

Yes, they do, Monica. But that doesn't mean you have to be the victim of them, even in the name of "love."

Listen: It is possible to "love" too much.

When being in love means being in pain, you are loving too much.

When most of your conversation with your close friends are about him, his problems, his thoughts, his feelings—and nearly all your sentences begin with "he . . . ," you are loving too much.

When you excuse her moodiness, bad temper, indifference or put-downs as problems due to an unhappy childhood and you try to "fix" it all, you are loving too much.

When you don't like many of his characteristics, values,

and behaviors, but you put up with them thinking that if you are only attractive enough and loving enough he'll want to change for you, you are loving too much.

When your relationship jeopardizes your emotional and spiritual well-being, and perhaps even your physical health and safety (as when a date tries to get you drunk, or insists on driving when he's drunk), you are definitely loving too much.

It's common, even applauded, in our society to "love too much" in these ways. Actually, it's not a case of truly loving too much; it's a case of being too dependent on another person. Maybe it's more accurate to say sometimes in a relationship we "need too much." When we look to the other person to make us happy, when being with the other person starts defining our reason for living, we've crossed the line from healthy to unhealthy love.

It's human to need love. It's good to need love. It's okay to need your boyfriend or girlfriend. But you can't depend on anyone else to create your happiness for you or provide your reason for living. And, if in a relationship a person is not giving you support and affirmation and respect, you don't *deny* your need for love by quitting the relationship. Rather, you *acknowledge* your need for love by ending that relationship and looking for one with someone who is capable of truly loving.

Monica confused several things in her own mind, and it led to an unhappy marriage. She recognized that she could not live without love. None of us can. But then she convinced herself that because she felt certain feelings when with a particular man, she must love him. And he said he loved her. She then equated her inability to live without love with her inability to live without this particular man, despite the fact that he didn't act very loving. If she had told herself, "I can't live without love," and thought about just what love is, maybe she would have seen—before she was married—that this particular person wasn't giving her that kind of love.

Maybe then she would have found love with someone else, before committing herself to a marriage headed for disaster.

*This material has been taken from the booklet *Top Secret* by Jennifer J. Fay and Billie Jo Flerchinger, copyright 1982, 1988, King County Rape Relief, 1025 S. Third, Renton, WA 98055.

**This material is from Claudette McShane, Assistant Professor of Social Work, Carroll College, Waukesha, Wisconsin.

BUSINESS REPLY MAIL

FIRST CLASS   PERMIT NO. 8182   DES MOINES, IA

POSTAGE WILL BE PAID BY ADDRESSEE

CAMPUS LIFE
Subscription Services
P.O. Box 11624
Des Moines, IA 50347-1624

18. *Breaking Up*

It started with a sick feeling in the pit of my stomach. I tried to tell myself I was just coming down with the flu, but I knew better. I didn't want to face the fact that I felt sick because I knew that my boyfriend was about to break up with me.

The signs had been there for a few weeks. A growing lack of interest and attentiveness toward me. And a growing attentiveness toward someone else. My best friend, no less.

So when Mark finally told me he wanted to break up, I should have been ready. I wasn't. We sat on the swings in my backyard as he said the dreaded words. I cried, but knew there was no use. He liked someone else better than he liked me now. We agreed we would "still be friends," but I wondered if that would be possible. Back in my room, I felt as if my world had fallen apart. I cried some more.

Breakups hurt. They hurt a lot. You feel like a failure. You feel rejected. Even if you're the one who initiated the breakup, you have to deal with feelings of loss, perhaps feelings of doubt about yourself and your ability to keep a relationship going.

But sometimes breaking up is the kindest thing to do, in the long run. If a relationship is stifling you, if you're just plain bored, if you're really more interested in another person, if you've outgrown each other, if your values clash, if you're moving away and you don't see the point of preserving a relationship—these and many other reasons are good cause for breaking up. And certainly, if the relationship is unhealthy—if there is jealousy, abuse, or an unhealthy dependency—the best thing to do is end it—fast! Even if there are still some feelings of love there.

BLAT!

RATHER THAN LEAD WALT ON, LOIS THOUGHT IT BEST TO BE UP FRONT ABOUT HER DECISION TO BREAK UP WITH HIM.

HOW TO BREAK UP

We all know in theory that the best way to break up with a person is in person. But that's much easier said than done! Too often we settle for sending the person a note, or we say it over the phone, then never see or talk to our ex again. One guy complained, "She just left me coldly, like an animal. It took a long time to get over the heartbreak." Even if your original attraction is gone completely, there's no reason to be cruel about a breakup.

The best way to break up is by gently telling the truth. If you still care about the person, show it by sitting down with him or her and explaining how you feel. Focus on your own feelings, not the problems with the relationship, and keep blame out of it completely.

If you know it's time to break up, don't put it off. It only gets harder the longer you wait, and it will only hurt the other person more.

And it's going to hurt. Accept that. You may be ready to be friends right away, but your ex may not be for a long time—if ever.

Carole found out how difficult a breakup can be, even though she initiated it. "Everything seemed to be going OK until he announced, out of the blue, that he has no desire to be my friend anymore," she says. "He never wants to see me or talk to me again. I'm feeling intensely hurt, because his decision was so sudden and I've never faced rejection like this before. I feel worse than I felt when we broke up, because I think now I've completely lost him. I don't know what to do or where to turn. I didn't realize how much his friendship meant until now."

Ideally, people ought to be able to stay friends even after the romance is over. Practically, that's not always possible. Sometimes it just hurts too much. Sometimes you need a long cooling-off period.

So what do you do if you'd really like to stay friends, as Carole did? One thing is to write your ex a letter. Explain that you're sorry for the pain, that you understand why the person would be angry. Remind your friend that you value the friendship and hope someday the two of you can be active friends again. Let the person know that you're willing when he's willing, if that day ever comes.

And then? Then leave your ex alone. God can give each of you other friends.

HOW DO YOU MEND YOUR BROKEN HEART? _____

It's very scary when you break up with someone after you have shared so much with each other. It's like they have a part of you which they can either preserve or rip apart.

—*College female*

After dating for a while and then going steady for three months, my girlfriend broke up with me. She is a wonderful Christian girl and I thought everything was great. Several months have passed and I still hurt. I pray almost continually about my feelings, but God doesn't seem to take away the pain. Is it normal to hurt like this, or is it that I'm just not trusting God enough?

—*High-school male*

When a relationship ends, a person ought to feel some pain. That's one indication that the relationship meant something. If you didn't feel some hurt, it would mean either you are a shallow or callous person, or that the relationship didn't go very deep.

There's an old saying, "Time heals all wounds." I didn't believe it, after the breakup of my first serious relationship. I didn't think I would ever heal. And even if time was the answer, how was that going to help me right then?

I eventually did find the saying to be true, but I would rewrite it: "A long, long time eventually heals all wounds." It took me quite a while to get over that relationship, a long time to trust myself to love again. I've found since that some things help speed up the healing process.

Allow yourself to go through the grief process. You've lost something—a significant relationship. When people experience loss, they grieve. People who have studied grief identify five stages.

First, there is denial. "I never really loved him." "She was really a jerk anyway. I'm better off without her." Denying your pain is an attempt to cope by rationalizing it away. But it doesn't help you to deal with your loss.

Denial can lead to trying to protect yourself. You decide you're not going to care. People who do this insulate themselves by treating everyone else and every relationship casually. I confess I did this for a while. I made sure that

180   *The Campus Life Guide*

other relationships stayed strictly on a "friendship" basis. While that can be a healthy thing to do until emotions heal, there is an inherent danger: You cut yourself off from future positive relationships.

A common male version is the guy who moves from one relationship to another putting notches on his belt. He conquers one girl and then goes out with another.

The female version is the girl who snags a guy but keeps him at a distance. As soon as he starts getting to know her, she finds some fatal flaw in him or declares herself bored with him, and she dumps him for another.

People who don't ever invest themselves in a relationship think they're avoiding hurt. But actually they're exploiting and hurting others. And slowly they're destroying their own chances of finding any healthy relationships.

Denial may be a natural first stage in the grieving process. But see to it that you don't let yourself get stuck there.

The second stage is anger. "I could kill him for making a fool of me!" "How could she dump me for that wimp?"

Ah, now we're getting to some honest feeling. You've been hurt, and you're angry. That's healthy—again, to a point. Let yourself feel the anger. Write it out, if that helps. Talk to a friend. Cry. Go out for a long run. Find constructive outlets for your feelings.

Two things to avoid at this stage: lashing out directly at the person who hurt you, or taking steps toward revenge (spreading rumors, doing something to "get back" at the person). Turn to others who understand, and let yourself hurt for a while.

The third stage is bargaining. "God, if you love me, bring him back into my life." Or, "Maybe if I show her how many other girls are dying to go out with me, she'll reconsider."

When bargaining doesn't work, grieving people fall into depression. "I'm not worth loving. No one will ever come into my life again." Or, "My life has ended."

When you're depressed, you need understanding and affirmation from a few close and trusted friends. Jill says, "I don't know what I would have done without Amy there when Brad and I broke up. She understood, listened to me moan and cry, and reminded me that I'm OK. Her love helped me realize I am lovable."

Depression is normal too, but you don't want to get stuck in it. You feel rotten about yourself, and if you focus on those feelings, you begin to believe them. But if you lean on God and people who love you, you should be able to move through the depression to the final step—acceptance.

Acceptance means you keep the old images and memories. You realize you've gained something from the relationship and even its loss; you are now a stronger person.

Three other things will help you move quickly and surely through the grief process toward acceptance:

1. Pray. When I returned to my room after breaking up with Mark, I cried my heart out. And I found myself also talking to God: "Why? I was so sure he would be the one for me—why did he break up with me?" I told God all about my confusion, and I felt like he was listening. After crying and praying, I felt peace, as if God were saying, "I hold your life in my hands. Trust me."

All through the grieving process, I came to God just as I was: angry at times, depressed at other times (so much so I sometimes doubted there was a God). And God rode through it all with me. I never felt he was telling me what some adults were: "You'll get over it. There are other fish in the sea, you know." The adults may have been right (they were, as it turned out), but I felt they weren't taking my feelings seriously. God did.

2. Cultivate other friendships. It's quite common, when you're in love, to spend all your free time with your boyfriend or girlfriend. But I'm sure you can see why that's so unwise: you don't want to invest yourself so much in one relationship that you are bankrupt if that relationship goes bust. Now is the time to renew old but still good friendships, and to cultivate new ones. With both sexes. Let the balm of

friendship, with its ready acceptance of you as you are, be applied to your wound.

3. Get involved with other things, even if you don't feel like it. The best way to get up when you're down is to get actively involved with life. What did you used to like to do? Start doing some of those things again.

When there is more than one thing we care about, more than one person through whom we are fulfilled and revitalized, then we cannot be destroyed—no matter how much we are hurt—by the loss of one relationship.

One more word of caution: It's best not to get involved in another relationship until the yo-yo of grief is under control. Wait until you've reached the stage of acceptance, and move toward another relationship without the impulse to jump into something heavy right away.

Until that time, work toward becoming a secure and happy and loving person without a special relationship. The test of our security is the capacity to enjoy being alone—to make the most of those times when we don't date. That's the focus of the next chapter.

19. *When You Don't Date*

It was Christmas break. I called my friend Debbie to see if she wanted to go out to a movie.

Her mother answered the phone. "Oh, Debbie's not here. She's out with Mike. Can I take a message?"

"Oh, no, I guess not. I just wondered if she wanted to get together sometime soon."

"Well, she's quite busy these days. She has a boyfriend now, you know." I'm sure her mother didn't mean to be cruel, but those words kept echoing in my ears.

"She has a boyfriend now, you know." And I didn't. I hadn't gone out with anyone steadily in a couple of years. So what's wrong with me?

It's hard to ignore the fact that people couple up. Every year, Valentine's Day reminds those of us who are "unattached" of our own lonely state. There are other times, of course: homecoming, prom, the special Christmas dance— all those events that call for a date if you want to attend. We're reminded when we call friend after friend to make plans for Friday night, and we're told, "I have a date that night." Such times can make you feel like everyone is going out with someone—everyone except you, of course.

It seems that way, but it's not quite true. In one recent *Campus Life* survey, about half of the respondents said they dated once a week to once a month; the other half said they dated only occasionally, for big events like proms, or not at all.

And even those who are going out with someone will,

more than likely, break up sooner or later. The truth is, during high school and college, most people are "unattached" much of the time.

The question is not really, "How do you handle it if you're not going out with someone?" but "What do you do about the times when you're not going out with someone?"

First, you have to deal with the feelings.

WHAT'S WRONG WITH ME?

There's the self-doubt that sets in. You wonder, "What's wrong with me, that no one wants to go out with me?" (If you've just broken up, the question is, "What did I do wrong, so that the relationship didn't work out?") You feel you have to blame someone or something.

Don, a high-school senior, blamed both himself and the dating system for his lack of dates. "I'm not the type of guy that it's 'cool' to be seen with," he says bitterly. "I'm not a football player; I'm a basketball manager. I'm not in the popular crowd; I'm pretty much a loner. I'm not flirtatious; I'm shy. I'm not Mr. Self-confidence; I'm sensitive and soft-spoken. I don't have Tom Cruise-like looks or a great body; I'm short, skinny, and I have to fight acne. I don't have an expensive car—a BMW or a Corvette—instead, I drive my brother's old Honda.

"People sometimes tell me that my problem is a lack of self-confidence, but what reason do I have to be confident? I got an indirect rejection last year from a Christian girl two years younger than me.

"People also tell me I'm too serious, but that's just the way I am—I don't know how to 'loosen up' and have a great, fun time. Acting crazy isn't my idea of fun—a romantic, quiet dinner and a movie is, but girls don't really care about that kind of thing unless it's with their dream football captain. Girls want to date football players, not basketball managers. Therefore, I don't date and probably never will."

We can call Don pessimistic. We can say he's exaggerating. But we're talking feelings here. And feelings can run away with you. They have a way of tearing at your self-confidence. They get you looking inside, searching for flaws that explain why you're "unattached."

John doesn't go out on very many dates. "I can count them all on one hand—with two fingers missing," he says. (Obviously he doesn't lack a sense of humor.) For John, rejection is familiar—and never ceases to be painful. "Before I found out that I could even talk to girls, I found out that I could be rejected by them. Perhaps it was the type of girls that I tried to ask out—mostly pretty and popular. It was easier to talk to the girls that I saw a lot. Being a sports fan and on my high-school photography staff did not hurt my situation. I knew at least four cheerleaders that I could stop and talk to (one of them had the most gorgeous brown eyes . . . she also had a boyfriend)." His final analysis of his situation? "I suppose it could have been my fault. It might have been my physical appearance or the way I acted: too eager."

Debbie, a high-school sophomore who is fairly popular, has a different problem: she can't seem to get a steady boyfriend. "Just like everyone else," she says, "I've had a few boyfriends here and there that didn't work out, but I can't seem to get a boyfriend for any longer than three weeks. Am I the only girl who feels this way, or are there other people in my situation?" she asks. I can assure her there are others. "I feel as if it's my fault that no one likes me, that somehow I'm scaring guys off. I really feel awful because most of my friends have boyfriends. Is something wrong with me?"

Is something wrong with me? That question is asked again and again. Carolyn, 18, says, baffled, "I've never had a boyfriend. I seem to have everything else in life, such as a wonderful family, good school grades, and good friends. But because of this situation I find it hard to accept myself." And Sarah laments, "I am 17 and have never had an official date. I'm beginning to feel . . . I really don't know. It's not rejection, because I've got plenty of good male friends around. I just feel different—kind of like everyone else is dating or had dated before, but me. Why can everyone else find a date and I can't? I'm not odd-looking; I'm pretty ordinary. Maybe I act too uninterested. I'm just afraid. I try to make sure that finding someone doesn't obsess me, but sometimes I just get so down. I'm too embarrassed to talk to anyone about this."

So far in this book I've stressed the importance of friendship. But I understand that friendship goes only so far; it's the addition of the Plus part of a relationship that qualifies it for the Dream. It's wired into us: we want to feel attractive to the opposite sex. Whether we're male or female, if we don't have someone of the opposite sex who has declared that we are special, our self-confidence is shaken. We think, *There must be something wrong with me. We feel alone.*

But maybe there's nothing wrong with me. Or with you. Maybe there's something wrong with how we approach the topic.

Maybe part of the problem is that we only think we're valuable if someone else—someone of the opposite sex—says we're valuable. Desirable. And the more the other person has of what the world says is valuable—money, good looks, nice clothes, popularity, etc.—the more weight that person's opinion of us carries. If the most popular, best-looking football player wants to go out with me, I must be something. If the cutest cheerleader wants to date me, I must be OK.

But if that's true, so is the flip side: If not even the most ordinary guy or girl wants to date me, there must really be something wrong with me.

This kind of thinking is all too common. And it's dead wrong.

But how do you combat this wrong thinking?

You have to shift your focus. Blink, and look at things in a new way. Gain a little perspective.

IS THERE REALLY SOMETHING WRONG WITH YOU?

First, take another look at yourself. Does the fact that you don't have a special relationship right now really mean there's something wrong with you?

"It hit me hard, not going out with anyone," says Donna, a high-school junior from Georgia. "I liked this guy, and I couldn't understand why he didn't like me. But I took a good look at myself, and I finally got to the point where I could say, 'If a guy doesn't like me, that's really not a problem. There's nothing wrong with me. I know I'm the best I can be.' I've gotten to the point where I can accept everything about myself. I found you have to accept yourself for who you are before anyone else can really like you. Once you do that, you can really believe, 'If a guy doesn't like me, then he's missing out; it's not because of anything I'm doing wrong.'" Donna was able to realize that things just didn't click between her and the guy she liked. Rather than assume something was wrong with her, she decided that that's just the way the situation worked out.

But getting to that point was a process for Donna. And a big part of the process was, as Donna says, "turning myself toward God." Knowing that God accepted her, knowing that God had a purpose for her, with or without a boyfriend, helped Donna arrive at that point of freedom where she could say, "If a guy doesn't like me, it's not because of anything I'm doing wrong."

Learning to feel OK about yourself even when there's no "special someone" in your life not only strengthens you as a person, but as a potential lover as well. If you need a relationship in order to feel complete, you're looking for the wrong thing. Strong relationships are built on what you have to give, not on what you need from someone else. Unattached times can be ideal for exploring interests and discovering what you as a unique individual have to give.

A SECOND LOOK AT THE DATING SCENE ─────

After taking a good look at yourself, give the whole dating scene a double take.

The fact is, lots of otherwise attractive, likable, worthy people don't date a lot. One person describes herself and her situation:

> I simply don't get dates. It's a mystery to me and to a lot of other people. I just can't seem to put my finger on the reason.
>
> I am not bad-looking. I am intelligent. People tell me I have a wonderful personality, and I try to be friendly to everyone. Still, no one asks me out. I've got to say that at age 22, this problem is nearly tearing me up. I have tried giving up on men altogether, but it doesn't work. I am so lonely. All my friends have boyfriends or are married.
>
> It's not that I have no male friends. In fact, my best friends are male. (This has not always been the case.) I am a Christian, and know of other pretty and friendly Christian girls in the same situation. What is the problem?"

Just what is the problem? At least part of it has to do with how the dating system is set up. It's hard to put a finger on— it's more than just looks or personality—but some people just seem more "date-able." I've observed that there's usually a segment of any school or group that dates, and I haven't been quite able to define why. Maybe some people get tagged early as "date-able," and that image follows them. Usually the qualities that make a person seem date-able are pretty superficial and have nothing to do with sustaining good relationships—but they do tend to screen some people out.

Another reason might be an imbalance in the ratio of guys to girls. All during my college years on a secular campus, there were about five girls to every one guy in my Christian group. It's not hard to figure out why I didn't date much during those years.

A little healthy self-evaluation never hurt anyone. Maybe

you are doing something wrong. But then again, maybe you're not. Maybe it's your situation.

Does that mean there's nothing you can do? I doubt it. I've seen too many instances where a person who hadn't dated for years ended up in a great marriage. I've also known people who dated a lot, were seldom without a steady, and learned nothing about how to have a great relationship. Those people ended up in some very unhappy marriages. It's how the "alone times" are handled that seem to make the difference.

HIDDEN OPPORTUNITIES

Many people have told me they've grown through the times when they haven't dated. Stacey found her self-confidence grew: "Last summer, my friends didn't want to go to the pool with me, and I didn't have a boyfriend to meet there; so I went by myself. At first I felt self-conscious about it. But as time went on, I felt good. I proved to myself that I was strong enough to go alone, that I didn't always have to be seen with a guy or even with my friends."

Scott also found new freedom socially. "I used to sit at home if I couldn't get a girl to go out with me or couldn't find friends to do stuff with me. But I don't do that anymore. I'll go out with a girl who's just a friend. Or sometimes I'll even go alone. My sixteenth birthday was on a Thursday, and the next night I wanted to go out and have some fun, but I couldn't find anyone to go with me. So I went by myself. I treated myself to a movie I wanted to see and had a good time. Sometimes I'll go to a football or basketball game by myself if no one's available."

Another girl, a senior in high school, says she used to feel "desperate" because she's never been asked out. But she has since radically changed her perspective:

> I used to lie awake at night, crying and silently screaming at God for his "cruelty" to me. I couldn't understand why he

was depriving me of normality. However, since then, I have come to thank God for his wisdom in this matter.

Three of my best friends are sexually active. I sat and cried with each of them a few weeks after their "first times," and prayed with each of them that they weren't pregnant. Don't get me wrong. They aren't 'bad' girls, and they don't take sex lightly. They are all good Christians who thought they were giving their most precious gift to the men they would marry. But sex is no promise of marriage, and all of these relationships are now history.

I don't judge my friends for what they did. I would have done the same thing a year ago. That is why I thank God for denying me a dating relationship all these years. I was able to learn from my friends' mistakes and intensify my relationship with the Lord. Now I know, without a doubt or a regret, that I will only experience the joys and wonders of sex when I am married.

My prayer now is that the Lord will place me in a relationship with a strong Christian when he feels we are both ready for a relationship based on his love; and that until then, God will enable us both to remain pure in thought, motive, word, and action. I wish I could let all desperate people know that they are definitely better off without a date on Saturday than without their virginity. They can spend this time getting to know the Lord and learning a definite lesson in patience!

This girl did not consciously choose not to date, but in retrospect saw some great advantages to her unattached years. Other people do decide quite consciously not to have a "special someone" for a while—for some positive reasons.

GOOD REASONS NOT TO DATE

Rick decided not to date much in high school—and didn't feel he missed a thing. "I saw those years as a time to build lots of relationships with different people rather than to get tied down to one person," he explained. "So I didn't have a girlfriend, but our youth group would go out a lot as a group. I found that a lot more fun and more comfortable. You get to know both guys and girls that way." As Rick found, not dating doesn't mean you're doomed to a life of loneliness.

Heather decided to pay the possible price for hanging onto her Christian values. "I've decided not to go out with anybody unless he shares my Christian values and moral standards—which meant that lately I haven't been going out with anybody. But that's better than the hassle of dealing with pressures I don't need."

A realistic view of the dating pressures affected Doug's decisions about dating. "I won't go out with a girl unless I know she shares the same standards I have, especially about sex and drinking. And to tell you the truth, I don't want to get involved with a girl now because of all the pressure. Once you have a relationship, there's pressure to get too involved. Sometimes pressure from the girl. Sometimes pressure from other guys, to 'score.' I don't need that right now."

Brent found that when he was dating, the girl wanted to get more involved than he did. "So now," he says, "because I'm not interested in a serious relationship, I just prefer to go out in groups or to go out with the guys."

Laura also realizes that now is not the right time for her to get too serious with anyone. "I'm not all that interested right now in having a boyfriend. I'm at a point where I have to be my own person. I see so many couples become so exclusive—they're like Siamese twins! I guess I'm rebelling against that sort of thing. I'm happy enough with my friends."

Lynn knew she needed some time to regain her own emotional balance before seeking another relationship. "After I broke up with my boyfriend, I found I wasn't ready to jump into a relationship right away. It feels kind of good to be free again, like anything can happen. And it's a time to catch up on some of the things I let slide when I was going out—like schoolwork and my friends!"

THE CHOICE IS OURS

Not everyone can always feel OK about not having a boyfriend or girlfriend. We may get lonely. And though friends may help fill the gap, still we want a special someone—someone of the opposite sex—to remind us that we're special.

Still we long for our Dream to be fulfilled.

But alone as we may feel, we have to remind ourselves that very few people are involved in a healthy relationship all the time. On the way to the Dream, most of us will have to deal with being "unattached" at one time or another. If we deal with it as an opportunity to get to know ourselves, other people, and God more deeply, we'll grow through it. We'll have more to contribute to a relationship someday. If we sit around and feel bad about ourselves, we'll get nowhere.

Renee has struck a balance, poised on faith: "I just concentrate on being the best person I can be, the kind of person God wants me to be. I'd like to be going out with someone now, but I know that you have to feel good about yourself first. When the time's right, somebody will come along." Renee is, I believe, on the right road toward her dream.

Epilogue: The Risk of Love

Love is risky business. I doubt there's a person alive who hasn't been hurt in a relationship at one time or another.

So, after all my talk of the Dream, I have to warn you: Your dream will probably never quite come true.

Let me explain. When we dream of our ideal relationship, we are dealing with just that—an ideal. We envision someone with whom we can share everything, someone who will always understand us, appreciate us, be on our side. Someone with whom we can always share body, soul, and spirit.

The truth is, no person—or situation—is ideal. No one person will always understand and appreciate another. I will let you down, you will let me down. How I handle it when you disappoint me will determine whether or not I can build a lasting relationship someday.

Here's a familiar scenario: In a flash of anger, you say something cruel. Your words cut me deeply, and I retaliate. Suddenly our relationship seems torn to shreds. What was once beautiful is suddenly ruined, and perhaps neither one of us even understands how or why.

It's common to end the relationship at this point. In my disillusionment I may decide, "I guess this isn't the right person for me after all." And I move on. I may find another person, someone who seems right. Then, again, something happens, the relationship spins out of control, and I am left wondering what happened to the Dream.

So maybe the next time, I lower my standards. Someone doesn't seem to respect me, but what else should I expect? I let go of the Dream, and settle for something much less than the perfect relationship I once longed for.

That would be tragic. A better scenario might work like this: Instead of ending the relationship with you after our angry words, I resolve to work it out. We try hard to figure out what happened, where we went wrong. In the process, we learn something about ourselves and each other. We grow. Whether we stay together in the end or not, we will have learned something important: that relationships are made between two imperfect people. We learn something about forgiveness, about individual differences that can be tolerated, even appreciated.

What I'm suggesting is: Hang onto your dream, but make sure you color it with a healthy dose of realism.

Coloring your dream real means: You expect to be hurt occasionally, and so you work at learning how to forgive. You realize how easy it would be to hurt others, so you make it a priority to watch your words and to use them only to build up. You realize how sex can skew the delicate balance of sharing in a relationship, and you work much harder at getting to know the person's mind and soul than you do getting to know his or her body.

And you accept that love is risky business. You can't make someone love you, much as you may try. You can't make someone else change, much as you might love him. You may take the initiative and be rebuffed. You may love someone who loves you, then rejects you. There are no guarantees.

Loving is a fine art, perfected through lots of practice. So you practice loving all kinds of people. To the extent you are a loving person, you attract other loving people into your life. Love begets love.

Don't ever give up your dream—but do refine it as you go. Let each relationship be one from which you learn, and to which you give your best. Determine to leave both yourself and the other person richer in some way.

And someday, it's quite likely that you will have the kind of relationship you're willing to commit your life to. That's well worth dreaming of, working toward and sacrificing for.